MORE PRAISE F

"*Cross the Line* should be read by all who are seeking solutions to our inner-city problems. It should become a reference tool for inner-city community leaders."

Major General (Ret.) Calvin Franklin
President & CEO
Engineering Systems Consultants, Inc.

"*Cross the Line* is a compelling spiritual autobiography with surprising candor and refreshing pastoral insights. This book will be a blessing to all Christians who have experienced bad times. McKinney's voice is that of one of America's great pastors and spiritual guides."

Robert M. Franklin
President, Interdenominational Theological Center

"*Cross the Line* is an inspiring book written from the trenches of the inner city by a gifted and visionary leader. Its biblical foundation challenges many of the old stereotypes about inner-city ministry. It is a tribute to the grace of God and His love for the downtrodden and lost."

Dr. Wayne Kraiss,
President, Southern California College

"Bishop McKinney is a dear friend of mine. His whole life has been tied to the urban community for which we both share a concern. *Cross the Line* reflects his heart, his life, his ministry, and his principles."

Dr. John M. Perkins
President, John M. Perkins Foundation
For Reconciliation & Development

"For thirty-five years George McKinney has attended the School of Ministry in the Inner City. That experience uniquely qualifies him to speak on the subject with wisdom and authority. Anyone else who would aspire to minister in the inner city would do well to read this book."

Pastor Charles E. Blake
West Angeles Church of God in Christ
Los Angeles, California

Cross the Line

George McKinney
WITH **William Kritlow**

THOMAS NELSON PUBLISHERS
Nashville
Printed in the United States of America

Published in Nashville, Tennessee, by Thomas Nelson, Inc., Publishers.

Unless otherwise noted the Bible version used in this publication is THE NEW KING JAMES VERSION. Copyright © 1979, 1980, 1982, 1990, Thomas Nelson, Inc., Publishers.

Scripture quotations marked NIV are taken from the HOLY BIBLE: NEW INTERNATIONAL VERSION. Copyright © 1973, 1978, 1984 by the International Bible Society. Used by permission of Zondervan Bible Publishers.

Library of Congress Cataloging-in-Publication Data

McKinney, George Patterson.
  Cross the line : reclaiming the inner city for God / George McKiney, with William Kritlow.
      p.   cm.
  ISBN 0-7852-7246-1 (pbk.)
  1. City churches.   2. City missions.   3. Church work with the poor.   4. Inner cities.   5. City dwellers.   6. Cities and towns—Religious aspects—Christianity.   I. Kritlow, William.
II. Title.
BV2653.M35   1998
250'.91732—DC21   97–37312
                                                                            CIP

Printed in the United States of America.

1 2 3 4 5 6 QPK 02 01 00 99 98 97

*To the intercessors and ministers of
reconciliation who are workers with God
for the redemption of the city.*

CONTENTS

Acknowledgments   *ix*

Chapter 1   Answering the Call   *1*

Chapter 2   The Mission Field Is
the City   *17*

Chapter 3   Satan Drew the
Line   *39*

Chapter 4   Racism, Rage, and
Rebellion   *55*

Chapter 5   The Heritage of the Black
Christian   *75*

Chapter 6   Why Not Let Someone
Else Do It?   *85*

Chapter 7   How to Share the Gospel
in the Inner City   *105*

Chapter 8   Do You Have a Gift
to Share?   *129*

Chapter 9   Praying for the
Inner City   *145*

Chapter 10   But What Can
I Do?   *167*

**Chapter 11 Trusting the Results
to God   209**

**Chapter 12 Love Will Cross
the Line   223**

About the Author   227

ACKNOWLEDGMENTS

I have been attracted to the city since my first visit to Memphis, Tennessee, at age fourteen. It was the large concentration of people that really captured my attention. I found that the city was as segregated as rural Arkansas where I was born and reared. It seemed that all the society was black and white. Only a few brave souls dared cross the line in an attempt to establish mutual respect and friendship. Upon my call to the ministry, I was aware that it was a call to prepare for a ministry of reconcilement (2 Cor. 5:17).

I wish to acknowledge the faithful and loving support of my wife, Jean, who carefully edited the manuscript. For forty years we have shared our lives, our hopes, our pains, our dreams. By God's grace we are bonded for time in eternity.

I wish to acknowledge the contributions of my parents, Elder George D. and Rosie McKinney, who introduced me to Jesus and nurtured me in the faith; my high school principle, Mr. Branch, who encouraged me to go to the university for a liberal arts degree and the seminary rather than take the shortcut to Bible college directly from high school; and Dr. Lawrence Davis, T. L. Cothran, J. B. Jones, my mentors at the University of Arkansas at Pine Bluff. I would like to thank Dr. Walter M. Horton and faculty and fellow students at The Graduate School of Theology at Oberlin

College who encouraged me to continue in the path of discipline, integrity, and critical thinking.

I also acknowledge my debt to President H. B. London Sr., the faculty and the California Graduate School of Theology for their godly influence as I was seeking "midcourse" adjustments in ministry. The California Graduate School broadened my theological horizon and added fresh insights for effective ministry.

I also express my thanks to Pastor M. H. "Dad" Hawkins of Toledo who gave me my first opportunity to practice ministry in the city; to Bishop U. E. Miller who ordained me and performed the wedding ceremony for Jean and me; to Bishop J. A. Blake who invited me to San Diego, California, and opened the door of opportunity to develop an urban ministry; and to all those persons who have prayed, sacrificed, cried, and rejoiced in our long journey toward obedience.

A special thanks goes to my ministerial and office staff: Elders James Mason, Charlie Clark, Lorenzo Littlejohn, Superintendent Jesse McKinney, Missionary Marvella Simmons, Elder Julian Smith for his technical assistance, and to Theresa Flournoy, Joyce Banks, and Evelyn Gonzalez for their secretarial support. A special thanks also to Janet Thoma and Todd Ross at Thomas Nelson Publishers who encouraged me to complete this project.

Special thanks to Dr. John I. Davis, Elder Ronald Randle, Elder Raymond Sweet, and Pastor Barbara Brewton-Cameron whose stories of tragedy and triumph are included in this book.

Finally, I am deeply indebted to Mr. Bill Kritlow whose strong faith and noteworthy gifts as a word craftsman made this project possible.

CHAPTER 1

Answering
THE CALL

Now the word of the LORD came to Jonah the son of Amittai, saying, "Arise, go to Nineveh, that great city . . ." But Jonah arose to flee to Tarshish from the presence of the LORD.

Jonah 1:1–3

When it comes to inner-city ministry, many Christians are like Jonah: they refuse to answer the call. And, I have to admit, there are times when I look out over the tall buildings and the decaying neighborhoods and feel like all goodness and all conscience have been scraped away, leaving nothing but base ugliness. No wonder God's prophets are tempted to turn and run. Yet I know God has not abandoned the inner city. Here's why.

In the fall of 1984, St. Stephen's Church of God in Christ, the church I have pastored since its founding, was twenty-two years old. In that time it had grown to more than 3,500 members. On Sunday there were five services and during the week any number of activities, some on television and radio, promoting the gospel of Jesus Christ. We had ministries that encouraged the saints and touched the lives of prisoners, drug dealers, gang members, prostitutes, and those at risk of becoming them. The Lord was blessing these ministries—thousands had been and were being touched by God's miraculous salvation.

By any measure we could take godly pride in what we had accomplished in the inner city of which we were a part.

One Sunday morning that September, thousands of worshipers were going to gather to celebrate our twenty-second anniversary. At 2 A.M., six hours before the service, my wife, Jean, and I couldn't sleep because of the heat and the anticipation. So we were sitting on our patio, trying to keep cool, when the phone rang. A moment later things got much hotter.

An anxious voice told us that St. Stephen's was on fire!

By the time I arrived, the church was engulfed. Red fire trucks, their lights flashing, their hoses strung everywhere, surrounded the place while an army of firefighters engaged in all-out war. The fire raged inside, thumbing its nose at us as it broke out of shattered stained glass windows and doors, gnawing at the walls and punching through the roof.

Other church members had arrived before me, and many more arrived after. Because the flames were so ferocious and the firefighters warred with equal intensity, we gathered across the street in an ever-increasing knot of worshipers to beseech God for direction, for courage, for comfort, and for support in areas we had yet to imagine.

I suppose I could tell you now how spiritually well grounded I was. How, even as the church I founded and nurtured for over twenty years was being devoured right before my eyes, I was confident that all would work out well, that instead of a disaster we were looking at the first step in a new beginning.

I wasn't.

I was frightened. Frustrated. Fatigued at the thought of starting over. For this was more than just our church going up in flames. This was a church whose school we had dedicated to the Lord not more than two weeks before. A church my congregation had literally fasted for. To raise the final money that completed construction on this facility, the members of my congregation had eaten only two meals a day for three years, giving the money saved on that third meal to the church. All that sacrifice now amounted to little more than a pile of ashes.

But worse than all the frustration and weariness was the fact that I felt betrayed by the very Christ to whom I'd prayed so often for protection. A verse in 2 Kings tells us that if God is watching over the camp, no enemy will prevail against it. Now, as I watched the flames taking down our church, I had to ask myself, Was God on watch? Had he turned his back on us? Had he decided we were no longer needed where we were? Had we offended him in some way?

It seemed that just as God had allowed Satan to attack Job, so he was allowing Satan to attack us. For, as surely as I stood outside the flames, Satan and his minions were at work on the inside. I could actually hear them roaring like enraged animals. Satan, ranting in the flames at the window—standing guard while his horde danced in a destructive frenzy inside, their claws and jaws tearing at the pews, at the walls, the floors, the pillars. While God, our hope and protection, stood by.

3

Ashes fell on us like black snow, some still hot, burning through my shirtsleeves, igniting my skin. I was nearly brought to tears when I remembered that the evening before I had been surrounded by that same wood and the deep aroma of wood oils and flowers. I had sat in the front pew of our six-hundred-seat sanctuary praying for the coming service. Had I known where I would be standing only a few hours later, I would have prayed for the resilience of those faithful hearts that now stood around me breaking. The fragrance of wood oils and flowers had vanished, replaced by the bitingly acrid scent of the ashes and our deep confusion and frustration.

Helplessly—as if watching our own children being devoured by lions—we saw St. Stephen's Church of God in Christ reduced to black, smoldering ashes.

"Remember the argument we had," one of the trustees said to me, soot streaking his face where the tears had run, "that one about the fabric color on the pews? Doesn't seem quite so important now."

I could only nod as I gripped his shoulder and gave it an affectionate squeeze.

By 3 A.M. the news services had arrived. They set up their vans on the outside perimeter of the fire trucks. Soon a few city leaders came to graciously offer what support they could. A national news service from Denver arrived later. Their reports were flashed as far away as Boston.

DREAMS TO ASHES TO DREAMS

At 8 A.M., while fire department investigators sifted through all our blackened hopes and visions for the future, we held the celebration service. It was as if I

4

had two hearts. One was celebrating with the others. That one rose to the heavens in song, praising the Lord for all he had done in the past twenty-two years: all the miracles he had performed through us within our neighborhood of poverty and disaffection, all the souls he had brought to himself—and the lives he had transformed, all the beauty he had fashioned from all of life's ugliness. Oh, how filled that heart was, how exhilarated it was as Jesus was praised in word and song.

But there was another heart.

As its brother floated to heaven, this other heart was leadened, desperate in its defeat.

It saw God's rejection. God's punishing hand. God's indifference as he allowed my enemy to triumph.

That heart became even heavier as the fire investigators told us a few hours later that the blaze was undoubtedly arson. One of Satan's own had torched our church. And he had done it when it would hurt the most. Through neglect, we were grossly underinsured, $250,000 under, which meant that we would, in all probability, have a very difficult time rebuilding. As that Sunday rolled on, I became increasingly aware that God was closing doors. As much as we can say that the church is not the facility but the people, the facility is so important in the ongoing ministry of the church that, without it, we would have to curtail many of our works.

I could feel that leadened heart begin to break.

And that's when the Lord began to show me what he really had in mind.

Before that day was out, several of the local churches—among them Lutheran, Methodist, Catholic,

Baptist, and Unitarian—had written us checks. An Episcopal church actually took $10,000 from their own building fund. Soon we had over $150,000 in donations to help us rebuild. God continued to speak to our congregation through his actions. A congregation who had seen their spiritual dreams literally go up in smoke were now seeing God fill their cups to overflowing. Not only did he provide money, but he also provided a series of facilities from which we could choose. A nearby church within our own denomination offered their facilities to us. So did the Catholic church less than ten blocks from St. Stephen's, and a nearby Jewish synagogue as well.

But, as it turned out, we did not accept any of those offers—God had something even bigger in mind. An evangelist had planned to visit our community but for some reason had to change his plans. So, instead of wasting something he'd already reserved, he provided us with a 2,000-seat-capacity tent, which we placed on our property.

What a blessing—a 2,000-seat tent replacing a 600-seat sanctuary. And what a sight that tent was. Boldly huge and snow-white, with flags emblazoned with Christian symbols flapping proudly at its spires. I was of one heart again, and it was filled to overflowing with love and gratitude to my Lord Jesus.

We put that tent to use too.

As you can imagine, the eyes of the community were on us. You could not get within a mile of that tent without knowing it was there. While those flags flew, we had services at least six nights a week. Not only did I and other members of the staff speak, but several evangelists visited and lent their majestic voices to

God's gospel message. Many, some as far away as Missouri and Kansas, came to preach, came to reach souls, came to use their ministries to raise additional funds for the rebuilding efforts. Our worship ministry expanded, and so did our ministry to the homeless. We allowed them to sleep under our tent at night, and several members of the congregation came nightly to cook and serve them hot meals.

Several weeks after the burning, a suspect was arrested. During questioning he admitted that "his god" had commanded him to burn down our church.

But, as God did with Joseph so long ago, he did with us now. What Satan had intended for evil, God had intended for good—great good.

From those ashes rose a new sanctuary, and a new dedication on the part of all of us to do the work the Lord had set before us.

The congregation, my staff, and I have learned many things because of this episode in our church history. The list of lessons is probably as long as the membership list. But there's one thing in particular I would like to share.

We were called to minister in the inner city in the early '60s. By 1984, with the emergence of the gangs, the drugs, the open and base perversions—all organized and void of conscience—many believed that God had handed the inner city over to Satan. That God had said, in effect, "If they want a life like that, I'll give it to them. Here, Satan, do your worst."

The first chapter of Romans seems to give some support to this position. Paul wrote that when people refuse to glorify God as their Creator, he gives them over to a debased mind (v. 28).

After the fire, had God allowed our ministry to wane, maybe even die, I would be the first to agree that God had abandoned the inner city. But God not only rekindled our light, he fanned it into a blazing flame—brighter—hotter—than ever before.

In a very real sense God reaffirmed his call to me, to all of us, in a loud and dramatic way, perhaps as loudly and as firmly as he possibly could except for an audible voice. By telling us he wants us flourishing here, he has said again, "Go to the city and preach."

But rebuilding our church is not the only evidence of his call.

It comes nightly on the evening news. It comes in the morning with the newspaper. And it comes every time you talk to other Christians about our schools and the direction in which our country is going. It comes in the form of news stories about gangs, about murder rates, about injustice, about wounded children and frightened youth. And it's a call to action, a call to ministry.

In the following pages we'll discuss what form that ministry should take, but make no mistake: just as St. Stephen's was being called to match the heat of that fire with the heat of our commitment—just as the King of Nineveh was being called to immediate repentance—just as any listener to the story of the good Samaritan is being called to love his neighbors—we are all being called to make a spiritual difference to those living in the inner city.

THERE'S NO TIME TO WASTE

There is an urgency to the call. Jonah sensed it. When God told him to go to Nineveh and preach, Jonah knew

God meant now. That's why he immediately headed off in the opposite direction. He didn't wait, like my children sometimes do, to be asked a second time. "But you didn't tell me to do it right now. I figured I had time."

Jonah knew he didn't have time. And when he found out what the Lord wanted him to say, the fact that he didn't have time was confirmed. He was to preach: "Forty days and Nineveh will be destroyed."

Marcus's story is just one example of the urgency of our call.

Marcus was sixteen and lived near St. Stephen's with his mother. I'd known him for years. He came to church with his mother, but their visits were infrequent. His mom's brother, Marcus's uncle, was a regular attendee. About six months before his mother came to see me about Marcus, his uncle moved from the city to a house in the suburbs and began attending another church there. When his mother finally came to me for help, she sat across from me in my office, her hands fidgeting with a tissue, her eyes troubled.

"He's getting mixed up with the gangs," she said. "I know it. There's nothing definite, but he's out late at night. He's disrespectful. He nearly gets violent when I come into his room unannounced. I know it's gangs."

She tore at the tissue more furiously, shredding it. Then her eyes rose. I'll never forget the fear I saw in them. A deep, resonant terror. A justified reaction. We've all seen what gangs do. The thought of your own son or daughter, the child in whom you've invested so much hope, so many dreams, hanging out the side door of a speeding van pumping bullets into some other mom's child—that thought is enough to strike terror into eyes of stone.

She went on. "My brother, Steve—you know Steve— he and Marcus talked sometimes. It all got worse when Steve left. Maybe you could ask Steve to talk to Marcus again. He'd listen to you."

There are so many fatherless boys in the inner city. In an effort to stem that tide, several of the men in our church mentor boys, becoming their advisers and friends. Sometimes in a very short time remarkable changes come about in these boys.

I called Steve.

"Pastor McKinney," he said, his voice restrained, "I understand your concern. But you have to understand—I've escaped. I've been able to get my wife and kids out of there. I don't want to subject my family to that again."

"But all I'm asking is for you to talk to him. See him, maybe once a week or so."

"I'm sorry. My life's out here now. I'm sure you can find someone else."

We didn't. Four months later Marcus was arrested for murder.

Opportunities are fleeting. Maybe the door is open for days, maybe only minutes or seconds. Sometimes only as long as it takes to load and slam home the first round in an Uzi.

But isn't the Lord in control of all this? If he wanted Marcus saved, wouldn't he save him?

Sincere Christians can differ on how involved they believe the Lord is in the events of our lives. Sincere Christians can also have different beliefs on how

involved the Lord is in orchestrating our
But none of us differ in our need to love c̣
bor. It's a commandment. One of the two most impoi-
tant commandments, according to our Savior. And
one way we show love is to hurry to the aid of the one
in trouble. When one of the saints is hanging by his
fingernails, you show love for him by running to help
him. It's not love if you see him hanging from his fingernails and you saunter up, whistling a happy tune,
with your hands in your pockets. "I'll be right there,"
you might say, "as soon as I chase this fly out of the
house."

There's no time for sauntering.

BUT WHAT ARE WE CALLED TO DO?

The inhabitants of the inner city are in trouble and
there's an urgency to help.

But it's an urgency to do what?

Some in the Christian community are primarily
concerned with solving social ills. They see the dev-
astation brought about by teen pregnancy and AIDS,
and they want to solve it by handing out condoms in
schools. They see lives shattered by violent crime and
they cry for more cops on the street. They see kids
ruining their lives, or ending them, with drugs and
they want to plaster bumper stickers on everything.
They want to keep kids out of gangs, so they push for
government programs to keep them busy.

No one is more concerned about these things than
I. But the solution to these problems will not come
through slogans and social programs. The solution
begins (and ends) with people coming to a personal,
saving relationship with Jesus Christ. Jonah was not

called to Nineveh to install a democracy or end child abuse. He was called to preach repentance. And it is through repentance, through walking humbly with Jesus, that individuals change for the better. People like Miguel, for example.

Miguel sold drugs. He did it in high school, and after dropping out he did it on a corner outside a Seven-Eleven, across the street from a brown stucco apartment building where many children live. In high school he sold it to the other kids: marijuana, coke, some speed. They would contact him via beeper and meet him where he had the stuff stashed, his car usually. He had regulars, kids who would hit him every morning before school and buy a few joints, a couple of packets. At first he'd be friendly with them. Joke around and laugh. He laughed a lot.

Then one of them died. A girl. She hadn't actually bought the stuff from him, but he knew her. Not well, but enough to remember her large brown eyes and rich, olive skin. She wasn't beautiful, but when she was around he had trouble keeping his eyes off her. Her boyfriend, some guy he knew only by sight, had mixed some heroin he'd gotten somewhere else with some coke he'd gotten from Miguel and made up a speedball. Speedballs killed movie stars John Belushi and River Phoenix. They killed the girl with the large eyes and olive skin too.

Miguel didn't joke around with his customers after that. He didn't joke around much with anyone.

Now, on his corner where he pays rent to some guy just to make sure nobody pushes him off the corner, there have been more deaths. Regular customers who suddenly have stopped coming around and have just as suddenly been featured in the street rumors as newly dead. These rumors are usually encased in nervous laughter. But death was not the only tragedy.

New customers sometimes arrived in suits. They pulled up to the curb in BMWs, Cadillacs, Buicks. They'd call out to him like they were calling to secretaries then drive away with pockets full of stuff. But before long the same customers would drive up in older cars; then they started arriving on foot, dressed in shirts and jeans, not suits. Miguel watched their lives ebb away, along with their eyes. When they were in the suits their eyes were bright, energetic, filled with life's challenge. But soon their eyes dulled. They became savaged eyes, seeing far less.

A lot of money passed through Miguel's hands. Most of it went to his suppliers, some to the corner-lord, but there was still a lot left over for his own drugs, alcohol, women, and gambling. It was the gambling that nearly cost him his life. In the drug business one has to be very careful only to spend the net profit. Because if you should miss a payment to a supplier, or to the corner-lord, your life might end violently.

When he missed the second payment to the corner-lord, Miguel found himself beaten nearly to death in an alley. The back of his skull was mush.

I met him when he was recovering. One of my church members suffered a brain tumor and ended up in the hospital bed beside Miguel. Fortunately, Miguel had health insurance.

Since the saint was laid up for a week, I had the opportunity to visit with Miguel. Then one night, after I finished reading a Bible chapter to the church member, I heard Miguel's strained voice. "Preacher. I done something God won't forgive. Anyway, what kind of God would forgive me for it?"

"A loving God. What did you do?"

"I killed a girl once. A beautiful girl. She's dead 'cause of what I done."

"All of God's people have done things they would give anything to undo. All of us."

"Is there really a God? If there is, he has to hate people like me."

The member went home after an operation (the tumor was benign) and soon Miguel went home. I visited him there on a regular basis, and one of the older ladies in the church went by periodically to help him clean house. It was she who had the distinct pleasure of winning his soul to Christ.

Miguel no longer sells drugs. Now, rather than ruining lives, he makes lives better, much like a gardener bringing beauty into the world.

But Miguel isn't the only example of social ills being healed by Jesus. One Friday night a number of our youth went into a particularly violent part of town to hand out tracts. Audrey remembers walking up to a grim-looking guy with icy black eyes and a stony expression. He sat at a bus stop, chewing a toothpick. Her heart thundering, Audrey handed him a tract. But he didn't take it. He just stared at her. His only movement was to switch the toothpick from one side of his lips to the other.

Wanting to do all she could, Audrey put the tract down beside him on the bench, then slowly turned and walked away. A week later at the Sunday service, the man appeared at the church doors. Eyes no longer ice, expression no longer stone, he boldly walked down the center aisle and laid a sawed-off shotgun on the altar. "I won't be needing this anymore," he said. That morning he gave his heart and will to Jesus Christ.

When Christ takes up residence in people's hearts, conscience appears and they begin to treat other people with love and respect. No social ill can withstand the onslaught of love and respect.

Well, in these first few pages we've covered a lot of ground: the reaffirmation of the call to minister to the inner city and how loudly it resonates in our hearts, that there's no time to waste, and finally, the focus of our message—the gospel of Jesus Christ. Our desire is to win souls to Christ. That was what Jonah feared God would do in Nineveh and what we want to do in the inner city.

But where is the inner city? And, aside from what we see of it on the six o'clock news—the murders, the bank robberies, the home invasions—what else about the inner city makes it a formidable mission field?

CHAPTER 2

The Mission Field
IS THE CITY

Arise, go to Nineveh, that great city, and preach to it the message that I tell you.

Jonah 3:2

Cities. The traffic, the buildings, the one-way streets that tie you in knots, the upscale apartments and town houses, the dingy and run-down 'hoods defined by red lines on banks and insurance company maps. Cities. Far from being abandoned, our Lord seems to have a special place in his heart for them.

Jesus lamented over the city of Jerusalem. "O Jerusalem, Jerusalem, the one who kills the prophets and stones those who are sent to her! How often I wanted to gather your children together, as a hen gathers her chicks under her wings, but you were not willing!" (Matt. 23:37).

The Lord allowed Abraham to barter for the entire population of Sodom and Gomorrah for as few as ten righteous souls. Of course, the Lord didn't find those souls, and he destroyed the cities.

The Lord sent Jonah to Nineveh to give it—"that great city," he called it—one more chance. Nineveh took it.

Throughout Scripture cities are mentioned prominently. The Lord commanded Paul to remain in Corinth, a very great city, because he had "many people" there (Acts 18:9–10).

The obvious reason cities are important to the Lord is because they are population centers. For an evangelist eager to present the gospel to as many people as possible, while spending as little energy and resources as possible, they're made to order. It only stands to reason that the Lord would have more of his people in New York, New York, than in Gallup, New Mexico. But I believe there's another reason they hold such a special place in his heart. The city, by its very nature a cafeteria of "need-satisfiers," blinds those living there to their need for Jesus. Therefore, in his eyes, they need him even more. You can sense it in his lament over Jerusalem. Our Lord speaks as an outsider.

That's how we feel, too, isn't it? Outsiders. And most of us are glad of it. We're all under the influence of the city to some degree; we all go there periodically for one thing or another. But our hearts' attentions are normally focused elsewhere.

In Jesus' time cities were well defined. A thick, fortified wall surrounded the city, and you could only enter it through gates. People were either inside the city or outside. But there was another wall, an invisible wall outside the visible one.

And that wall still exists today. It's the wall of influence.

THE MISSION FIELD IS THE CITY

If you live inside that invisible wall, your heart's focus more often than not is on the city: what it does and what it provides. Outside the wall the opposite is true. Since there are no fortified walls surrounding Los Angeles, or Chicago, or any other of our great cities, it's this invisible wall that defines the city today, defines it for everyone living on the outside. And, as we approach the city, we know when we're passing through its invisible gates.

Most of us have driven through a large city. We've gone there on business, or to take care of some government issues, maybe to the theater or a sporting event. We've gotten on the bus or train, or climbed into the car and taken ourselves there.

What was it like for you?

Before actually taking up residence in the inner city, for me it was always just a little tense.

First, just seeing the tall buildings out there on the horizon is sort of like seeing the iceberg waiting for the *Titanic*. Then, as I near, the traffic tightens. Even after rush hour, the roads are thick with cars and buses. And they're all indifferent to me and where I want to go. None of them care a whit, and if they did there isn't much they could do to help. The closer I get, the more the confusion. Signs and off-ramps. One-way streets. The growing fear that I really can't get there from here. If I make a wrong turn, how will I ever find my way back? If I'm taking public transportation, what happens if I miss my stop? The anxiety level grows pretty quickly, pretty high.

The city, going into it or living in it, is not for the faint of heart.

But it's more than just a place put there solely to increase my blood pressure. For all too many the city is a seductress, a messiah, and even a prison.

THE CITY AS SEDUCTRESS

Gene, a Christian friend, has a wife, Jenny, and two lovely daughters, ages five and three. They are, by any measure, a loving family. They can't find their refrigerator for all the kids' artwork. Both baby books are completely filled, even to the footprints and the first little pink ribbons they taped to the girls' little bald heads. Gene got up with his wife for every two o'clock feeding—well, not every single one, but most—and he changed a goodly number of diapers. He sent Jenny flowers once just because it was Tuesday; he has never forgotten a birthday or anniversary. He feeds emotionally on everything his kids do, every developmental step, every clever little thing they say. And he adores Jenny—everything about her.

Gene works for a large computer company and was promoted a few years ago. Before he could assume his new duties, he was required to attend a ten-week school in a nearby city, one of the largest. Because he would be working long and often odd hours, he was also required to stay in the city during the week, only returning home on some weekends.

The instant he heard about the school, it felt as if his heart had been injected with lead. Ten weeks. It might as well have been an eternity. He actually thought about turning down the promotion.

"We're going to be married for fifty, sixty years," his wife said, trying to convince herself as much as console him. "Ten weeks won't be that bad. It will be horrible, of course, but not all that bad. Will you call me a lot? Oh—"

Her expression suddenly dropped even farther. "What about Deni's dance recital? It's in two months." Denise, their five year old was taking ballet and was suffering from confidence problems. "You won't be back by then. It'll break her heart."

"I'm sure I'll be able to work something out," he said. "And if I can't, I'll just come. I know where my priorities are. And I'll call at least five times a night." Then he pushed a playful finger in her face. "And you have to videotape everything, even when they're asleep. They look so cute when they're sleeping."

Well, he consoled himself on the drive up, *at least there'll be plenty of time to read my Bible.*

The company installed Gene, along with two other guys, in an upscale apartment in an upscale part of town. That first night there, he did call home five times, and the next morning he did read five chapters in his Bible.

He could walk to and from class, a circuitous route that took him through this building and that, over this terrace and through that shopping area. Within a day or so he had found several places to shop for the kids and his wife. He also found a few places to shop for himself. Nice places, places that catered to the up-and-coming executive.

Before Friday came he was down to calling twice a night—when the kids went to bed, and when his wife went to bed. He was down to reading only one chapter in his Bible, and Friday morning he missed reading altogether, although he promised himself he would read two chapters the next morning at home. He didn't. And he'd wandered two blocks in every direction. He found restaurants that catered to every taste and mood. He found coffee, frozen yogurt, candy shops. An all-night drugstore, a grocery store, a comedy club, and a fitness center, one a little larger than the one in the apartment building. Though the one in the apartment did have a Jacuzzi and sauna.

But even with all the possibilities outside, he did stay in now and then—and watched any one of nearly fifty cable channels. And if he couldn't find anything on TV, he walked to a movie complex that showed six films; it was only three blocks away. Or he'd go to the little "art house" nearby that showed mostly foreign films. If he preferred live entertainment, there was a coffeehouse with a guitarist in one direction and one with a flutist in the other. Both were open till 2 A.M. And if those were too sedate, there was a livelier place, with a band, a few blocks away.

After the second week lunches were spent at a sidewalk café, people watching. Existing in their own little worlds, the people scrambled here and there, sometimes rudely, sometimes like their brains were in the "off" position—walking one direction, stopping, walking another direction, cursing to themselves as if forgetting what they'd already forgotten and remembered twice already.

At least twice a week there was some kind of a crime to watch, someone screaming about a purse being snatched, or a robbery. Once a bank alarm sounded and before he could bring his cup of coffee down, sirens blasted around a nearby corner. Gunshots were fired. One buzzed by him like a hornet as he dived off his chair, banging heads with a waiter who was doing the same thing. The danger gave him a rush.

Once a bus went out of control and plowed into an open trench, where they were repairing the subway. From their classroom window he could see the police and rescue units struggling for at least an hour to get the passengers out, and then the cranes straining to lift the bus back onto the pavement.

On Wednesday of the sixth week the trainees were given time off from noon until 1 P.M. the following day, so those who lived close by could go home and spend time with their families. Instead of going home, all three roommates decided to grab a quick cab to the theater district where three Broadway-caliber plays were running. They went to the *Show Boat* revival, then to a comedy club.

On the seventh week Gene had to be reminded that Deni's recital was the next week. By then he couldn't bear to leave, even for the one night. He made up an excuse: a big project that the regional VP was involved in, "so I just have to be here. I have no choice." Then feeling relieved of all responsibility, he sat down with that day's newspaper, a Drambuie liqueur, and got ready to watch the sun set from the twenty-fourth floor of the apartment building, a sight he'd grown to dearly love.

About the time he finished the headline story, he suddenly realized the despicable thing he was doing.

He got to the recital only a minute or two before his daughter went on. When she came on stage and saw him there, she smiled at him: one of those huge, loving, relieved smiles that tingles all the way down to the bottom of a parent's heart. He praised God for waking him up in time.

Gene stayed at home that night. He confessed to his wife what he'd been thinking and feeling, and a gracious God gave her all the right words of forgiveness and love.

The next morning he returned to class—late—and told his instructors the unvarnished truth.

To the company's credit, Gene's input helped lead them to the decision to shorten the class and make more of it home study.

He gladly went back to calling his wife five times a night and reading his Bible every morning. But he had to admit, as he was packing to leave, that a part of him was sad.

He had grown used to being able to get anything he wanted, whenever he wanted it. He had grown used to the flutist, used to the restaurants, used to the fitness center, used to the movies—and the easy access to it all. Used to the vanilla nut café mochas and the rich almond scone he had every morning. He could easily see that the city and everything in it had become his focus.

Until that eighth week, everything else, including his family, had become an interruption. Gene could imagine what would have happened to him had he spent a year or two years there. All the shops, the restaurants, the cable channels, the job that kept him there, would have become all he thought, talked, and cared about. And, paradoxically, he would not have thought he was giving anything up, rather, he would have been gaining. But in reality, the opposite would have been true.

Now this little story ends happily. After all, "All things work together for good to those who love God, to those who are the called according to His purpose" (Rom. 8:28). But what if my friend had been a weaker man? What if Christ had not meant so much to him? What if his ego and the desire for self-gratification had won? The city would have pulled him away from everything important to him and to the Lord.

The city would have seduced him.

THE BEST AND THE WORST

In a secular world any number of people are all too eager to be seduced by the idea of getting the best a civilization has to offer anytime they want it. Can you imagine Caesar living in the country? And, as it was with Caesar, even more seductive is the idea of getting more of it than anyone else, actually proving yourself more worthy than the others in the pack.

But that kind of seduction has a price.

It takes a healthy income to live in the upscale sections of the city. What jobs provide that kind of money? Those requiring education, skill, and responsibility.

An architect friend lives with his accountant wife in a nice condo not all that far from the city center. He has become renowned for designing high schools, spending countless hours of research and study to come up with designs that are both efficient and resistant to vandalism. (It's amazing what kids can do to a hallway nowadays.) But he also wants to influence certain regulatory agencies. Their regulations can make—or cost—his projects millions, making him more—or less—competitive. To that end he belongs to several social and fraternal organizations and has even been the Commodore at a local yacht club.

Like the architect, most who have "made it" in the city perform their specialties well, while, at the same time, they're promoting and achieving their own personal goals.

When you have millions of people competing for jobs, money, power, prestige, and the need to be content and fulfilled, each with different talents, you have millions of people striking out in all directions—physically, emotionally, spiritually, technologically—and in all disciplines.

Will a musician who thinks he can make it big be content to stay in a small-town orchestra, or will he audition in a bigger city, with an eye toward an even bigger one next? When he finally gets there, he'll discover that he not only needs to play his instrument well, but he needs to play two or three other instruments just as well.

The city, because it offers the most to the best, will gather to itself exactly that—the best. The best in a myriad of different fields.

Criminals with an eye to hitting the big time won't stay in the country either. Just as the cities draw the best architects and doctors, they also draw the most ambitious, most vicious criminals; the others just don't survive. When the best in any field compete with one another, they only get better, or, in the case of the criminal, more vicious and unrelenting. And, as the combatants improve, the competition becomes more fierce.

The city becomes a professional battleground, and, like any battleground, those who succeed are the smartest and the strongest; those who succeed for long periods of time are smarter and stronger still.

And they know they are.

Egos balloon. The winners are flying high, at the top of their professions, making a fall doubly disastrous. Not only do they lose the "perks"—the privilege, the money, and all that money can buy—but their massive pride is crushed as well.

Being seduced by the city can also cost the soul.

With prestige, money, and pride on the line, the battle can become dirty, mean, and illegal. Doing the right thing can quickly be traded for doing whatever it takes. Ethics can just slow you down. The stakes are so high, it's imperative to achieve the advantage, no matter what road must be traveled. But we all know that. We've seen the news, the movies, and the television shows depicting it.

As in any high-stakes battle, the focus of the participants is only on the battle and the prize. My architect friend goes from bidding a job, to working the job, to bidding the next one. The musician goes from rehearsal to performance to another rehearsal. The cabdriver goes from fare to fare, stopping only long enough for meals—or maybe he just eats on the go. While the combatants are engaged in the battle they don't have time to think about much else. Their struggles are in the city, and nothing else matters.

Now, as on any battlefield, the troops are ranked and there are a lot more privates than sergeants, than lieutenants, than generals; but, as the battle ebbs and flows, everyone finds his or her place in it. Or he or she leaves.

We can only imagine what those battles were like when God called Jonah to a city like Nineveh.

But something else was probably going on in Nineveh that goes on in our large cities too.

Because of the huge populations, no matter what your taste in anything, you'll find others who have that same taste, no matter how lofty or perverse. Those with the lofty tastes know their tastes are lofty. They know they are the elite when it comes to knowing what is good. But those with the perverse tastes—and frankly I have no desire to list them here—also know they are perverse. Unlike the lofty, however, they don't want to think themselves perverse. They want to think themselves normal. The city offers a unique opportunity to do just that. No matter what the perversion, they will find enough of their own kind that they can convince themselves they are normal by the evidence of sheer numbers.

And so the city provides the best and the worst that a civilization has to offer. And it provides both in abundance. And those seduced by either—or both—look only to the city for what they want and need.

THE CITY AS MESSIAH

A messiah is a deliverer. One who takes you from a hell to a heaven. The one you turn to when you're in need. The one who provides. The one in whom you invest your future.

We've just seen how the city fills that role for millions. No matter what you want, you can get it from the city. If you have a problem, the city will solve it. If you're ill, the great medical centers will come to the rescue. If you're broke, some city program will help you out. If you have trouble with your kids, some social worker will give you advice. If your car breaks down, a bus will be along soon.

Now throw Satan into the mix. What is his mission? To turn our spiritual eyes on anything but Jesus. When he's got something as enticing as what the city can provide, his job is made easy. And that means our job is made more difficult. Jacques Ellul, a noted French theologian and sociologist, observed in his book *Perspectives on Our Age* (Seabury Press, 1981), "The city is man's attempt to find security, power, purpose, and meaning apart from God."

Except for being apart from God, that's the very definition of a messiah.

For us as Christians, of course, Jesus Christ is the Messiah. He is our deliverer. He takes us from the hell of not knowing God to the heaven of knowing him. His work saved us from eternal separation from God—from hell. After living a sinless life, he died on the cross for our sins, suffered the equivalent of an eternity in hell, then rose on the third day to sit at the right hand of God. He intercedes for us with the Father and at the resurrection on the last day he will present his people to God the Father, his Father, our Father. Then we will spend eternity with him in heaven.

Now that's what I call a Messiah!

But why is it important to understand that some see the city in the role rightfully belonging to Jesus? Because it's something we have to consider when we minister to the inner city, and it's what partially holds the inhabitants prisoner.

THE CITY AS A PRISON

I struggled for a while trying to define the inner city. I tried to come up with something that included socio-economic issues, or crime issues, or issues concerning broken homes. But it got all tangled up. And there's really no reason to get all tangled up. Because you know where the inner city nearest you is.

The inner city is the place you won't go, not even if your life depends on it. It's where, if you make a wrong turn and end up there, especially at night, you spin that wheel around and slam the gas pedal to the floor. You get out! That's where the inner city is.

But I want to look at the inner city a little differently.

I want us to look at it in terms of the people who live there.

TANYA

Tanya is fourteen. She has been sexually active since she was twelve. Now she has a baby, little Josh. Josh takes a lot of work and Tanya, a child herself, is often overwhelmed. Her mother, Shirley, lends a hand when she can, but Shirley works. Shirley's husband split years ago, so Shirley is the only support the family has.

During the day things go pretty well. Tanya is in a special class at school that allows her to bring and care for the baby while Shirley works.

But at night things get pretty tense.

Josh is not a quiet baby. He cries a lot and there are times early in the morning when Josh is just impossible.

Shirley's patience finally ran out one day. She sat her daughter down and told her that if Josh woke her up one more time, Tanya and Josh would be asked to leave.

"But there's nowhere for us to go."

"That's not my problem. I got to work—I got to earn money to keep you and Josh in diapers and Gerbers. You're the one that got knocked up, not me. One more time and you're out."

I work closely with the police in our neighborhood. Sometimes, when they're faced with an incident they believe requires a gentle, spiritual touch—or one where they're not sure how they should react beyond doing the obvious—they call me. At 6:30 one morning Jean answered the phone and immediately pulled me from the shower.

At three that morning, Tanya, faced with Josh's crying and her threatened expulsion onto the streets, had done the only thing she could think of to silence him: she superglued his mouth shut. And, to make sure he fell back to sleep, she did the same to his eyelids.

Josh survived, but not without permanent eye damage. The extent is not thoroughly known.

KURT

Kurt is a heroin addict. He's been on "horse" off and on since he was twenty-two. He's now thirty-four. He had remained clean all the way through college, where he majored in civil engineering. Kurt's dream was to build the equivalent of a bridge across the Grand Canyon. It didn't actually have to be across the canyon. It just had to be something that magnificent. Across the Amazon maybe, or Niagara Falls, so people could walk up there and look down upon the rushing waters.

At his graduation party, one of Kurt's fraternity brothers brought some heroin.

He thought it was a lark. A walk on the wild side. No, not a walk. A few, fun little steps. After all, they were young adults. They had their lives ahead of them, and trying something like this was just part of the smorgasbord they wanted to taste.

It would be an adventure.

It was. Almost the instant the needle penetrated the skin. An incredible burst of razor-edged sensations. A feeling so intense, so all-encompassing.

When he came down, though, it was the opposite of the intensity. A dullness. A bleak sense of nothingness. He'd seen the brightest lights and now he was being cursed by senseless gray. Yet, in its own way, this lack of intensity, this ravaging dullness, was every bit as intense as the needle had been. But it was a far different intensity; embedded at its core was a hunger.

Kurt lasted two days before he got high again.

This time when he came down, he knew he was in trouble. The hunger was as consuming as the high had been. He had smoked for a few years in high school. When he had finally quit, he craved cigarettes all day long. He would try to read, or watch television, or breathe, and he'd have to push the craving away, but it was like pushing away a fog. Fortunately, his willpower prevailed.

The craving for the heroin made Kurt's craving for a cigarette feel like a mild desire.

He lasted nearly a week before he gave in again.

Kurt never built a bridge. He did get a job with a city, and kept it about a year, but when he was busted for possession he was fired. Sentenced to rehab, he looked upon it as a chance to get his life back. He went through the program, found another job, got some money—and got high again.

Over the years a couple of women fell in love with him. Each gave him up. The last one about a month ago—after being with him for nearly two years. Now, with half his life gone, Kurt works for a few weeks at a time, deals some on the side, but hates himself when he does. He earns just enough to keep himself using. He's been through program after program, and as he goes through each one he hopes this one will be the one that changes his life. But it never does.

He's lost so much time that he'll never retrieve— so many experiences—so many bridges he'll never build. So much love he'll never have or give. In spite of his dramatic highs and the canyon lows, Kurt was a flatliner—a patient with no heartbeat.

CARL, KATHERINE, TISHA, AND BRANDON

There is nothing like the color of blood on cement. And there's nothing more crushing to the heart and the spirit than to know that blood is your son's.

Carl, just twelve years old, was shot dead in the late afternoon. He had taken a shortcut down an alley, and the police figured he got in the way of two gangs fighting over some disputed turf. No witnesses saw it. But people heard the shots. A bunch of them. And when the firing was over, Carl lay on the pavement, his blood in a grotesque pool.

33

Katherine went out to see her boy's blood twice. It lay inside the yellow police ribbons.

A friend finally brought her back home.

Katherine found Tisha and Brandon, Carl's seven-year-old sister and fourteen-year-old brother, in the front room. They were reacting to Carl's death in dramatically different ways.

Tisha sat on the floor, her back pushed against the sofa, in tears. Heaving, stormy tears. Normally Tisha is not an emotional child, but this was not a normal moment in her young life. Her brother, the brother who had been as much a part of her as her heart, was gone.

Brandon sat in the old overstuffed chair, his feet dangling over one arm, his back against the other—cradled there. No tears. Iron eyes. Iron jaw. His mother could see his hate actually growing there.

She could do nothing for either of them.

On the way home she had relived what she imagined her son's last moments were. That instant when he knew he was about to die. When he saw the gun leveled at him. When he felt the slug slam into his chest. A lot of things in the neighborhood could scare a boy of twelve, and her son had often been scared. He usually went nowhere alone. But for some reason he had been alone in the alley. He must have been terrified. And she couldn't comfort him. She couldn't help him. She couldn't be his mother—anymore.

And now, standing there at the door to her living room, she couldn't be a mother to her other kids either. She was drowning. She had been given more than she could possibly handle. So, instead of scooping her daughter into her arms and shielding her from

34

a hostile world, she collapsed on one of the dining room chairs and dropped her head in her hands.

When her face came up, Tisha stood at her side, a hand patting her shoulder, while she asked if her mother was all right. Katherine finally hugged Tisha.

As the weeks unfolded, Katherine's heart developed a dead spot. Tisha watched a lot of television and seldom played with her friends. She started climbing in bed with her mother in the middle of the night. At first Katherine took Tisha back to her own bed, but now she just lets her stay. The dead part of her heart is too heavy to move at night.

Brandon began to stay out late at night. He was never a particularly easy kid, but now he developed a bitter attitude. The same friend who had helped Katherine home from the bloodstained alley that terrible night suggested that Brandon might be getting involved with the gangs. "You have to do something, Katherine. Confront him—tie him to the bed—do anything you can to keep him from the gangs. Once they have him, they'll never let go."

Katherine did confront him, but with her own heart dying, it was a halfhearted confrontation. Brandon admitted that he was getting involved with the gangs, but for only one reason: he wanted revenge.

Katherine said something she thought was uncharacteristically clever. "The gangs are like those Chinese puzzle things—you push your fingers in pretty easily, but you can never pull them out. They'll hold you captive forever."

Brandon responded like a typical kid. "At least I'll be doing something. Not like you. Carl was my brother. Somebody's gonna pay for him."

Katherine could find nothing else to say. She needed more heart to fight harder. But there was something else working on her. Brandon might actually get his revenge—and she wanted revenge too. She finally said something a mother might. "Looks like I'm going to lose you too."

That night when Tisha crawled into bed, Katherine rolled over and wrapped her arms around her, hugging her tightly—as if clinging to the only reality she knows.

CONFUSED AND ENTANGLED

Can you imagine any of these people leaving the city? They're not so much trapped there as they are entangled, their emotional roots wrapped up in what their environments offer them. Now each could extricate himself or herself, but the will isn't there. They actually believe they're doing what's best for themselves. They all see their "salvation" coming from the wrong place. They are all truly confused.

We know that Tanya, the young lady with the Superglue, could use the love and instruction a less demanding environment can offer. She's terrified. She's fourteen with a baby and there's no one to help. She has all the responsibility with none of the knowledge or power, so she reacts any way she can, no matter how irrationally. The tragedy for Tanya is that she sees no salvation at all; there's no one to come to her aid, no one to make the pain of her situation go away. But, on the brighter side for her, while in the city, there's no one to condemn her either. In a smaller town, there might be any number of people who would try to take over her life.

Kurt is lost in the forest of heroin. When he breaks from the trees and sees daylight, he turns and wanders back until he's lost again. He is destroying himself—a slave to his fear. As long as he's lost in the forest, he's not responsible for what's happening on the outside, in that part of his life that could be normal. Being lost is his salvation. He needs a city to get lost in, a place where he's just another life passing by. In a small town, he would be too visible.

Finally, Katherine. She's looking to her own emotions for help, and as long as they fail her, she doesn't have to go forward and face her other responsibilities. Brandon is looking to his own wiles, his own strength, and finally, to the support the gang will give him. Tisha is only seven, but so far everyone around her who should be supporting her isn't. There will come a day, if Katherine remains in her cocoon, when Tisha will look for support elsewhere. In the city, she'll find it.

You can only imagine how their lives would change if suddenly they looked to Jesus for their salvation, their deliverance, the meaning for their lives. Their confusion would end. Their eyes would focus. Their paths would straighten.

Our job, of course, is to present Christ to them.

But that's the challenge of inner-city ministry, isn't it? To present Christ, we have to get into their world. On the surface this sounds like a simple matter. Finding the inner city isn't all that difficult. Thousands of accumulated miles of concrete lead there. But there's another obstacle in our way. One that can easily subvert all the concrete and all our good intentions. In the next chapter we will talk about that obstacle.

CHAPTER 3

Satan Drew
THE LINE

And should I not pity Nineveh, that great city, in which are more than one hundred and twenty thousand persons who cannot discern between their right hand and their left?

Jonah 4:11

Audrey, one of our teens, went out with the youth group to hand out tracts at a local park, one known as a drugstore. It takes courage to do something like this, and we're never sure of the return. The faces we see are always changing and we never know if the tracts are even read. This particular morning, though, Audrey knew that at least one of her tracts was not.

A boy about her own age sat on a small curb that circumscribed a play yard. Since he was sitting near the ground, his knees were pulled up and his chin rested dejectedly on them. His vacant eyes stared straight ahead. Maybe he was deep in thought, maybe he wasn't. With swings rhythmically squealing in the background, Audrey stepped up and pushed a tract at him. It took a while, but he finally looked up, eyes still deep wells. Then a hand came up and he took the tract. As we always do, she said, "God bless you," and turned away. While handing a tract to someone else

39

nearby, she saw something out of the corner of her eye. An older man, someone the boy probably looked up to, walked up to him, grabbed the tract, and ripped it up. As he threw the pieces to the ground, Audrey heard the guy say, "You don't want that—it's trash— nothin' in there but lies."

There are two explanations for the older man's reaction. First, the man had no idea what was in the tract and it didn't matter. He just knew he hadn't put it there and since he hadn't, he saw it as a threat to whatever he had in mind for the boy.

Or, perhaps he'd been told or had seen firsthand the saving power of the words in that tract, and salvation for the boy was also a threat to the man.

In either case he viewed that tract with deep suspicion and had no intention of allowing it into his world.

That day Audrey had bumped up against the wall, an obstacle that keeps our ministry from being a simple matter of physical distance. I've talked about that wall before, the one that surrounds the community of the inner city. Of course, it's not a physical wall. You can't see it. But like the winter cold, you feel it when you cross the line.

As we've just seen, this wall also surrounds the individual, like a membrane, keeping the person safely within the status quo—no matter how disagreeable it is.

MY NONSCIENTIFIC SURVEY

Recently I conducted a little survey in my neighborhood. It was nonscientific. I just asked a question of people at random, taking the first answer that bubbled up. Our neighborhood had ten murders in the month of January 1997. Some were just innocent victims. Plus there's other violence—gang assaults, domestic explosions—and drug sales and use everywhere. By all definitions, our church is in the 'hood.

The question I asked was this: "With all the good reasons to leave the 'hood, why do you stay?"

These are the relevant replies. (Now remember, people are dying, some of them children, in significant numbers.)

"My job's here."

"My mom's here. Who would baby-sit for me?"

"I've lived here all my life."

"My people are here."

"I couldn't get a job out there."

"The kids' friends are here."

"The problem's here and I'm not going to run from it."

"Couldn't afford to live out there."

"Whitey's got me in a box. He ain't going to let me out."

"I know where everything is here."

"I'd be abandoning my people."

"This ain't so bad."

"Nobody's forcing me to move. Nobody."

SURVEYED IN SUBURBIA

Then I asked one of my white friends to do the same thing in the suburbs. He asked: "With all thc problems of the inner city, why don't we help the people living there?"

These are some of the answers:

"Walk around anywhere near there and I feel like I'm going to be attacked."

"I feel like a real outsider."

"Why should I?"

"If it's so bad that they need help, they can leave."

"People ultimately do what they want. They probably don't want my help."

"I don't have to go. My money's already there—in welfare."

"If they're dumb enough to live on a minefield—"

"I don't see how I can do anything the government's not doing already."

"I'm responsible for my life. They're responsible for theirs."

"I'm no good with them. I try to be friendly, and they just shut me off."

"My heart goes out to them, but I've got my own family to support."

"You read about those guys, right? They took the wrong turn and ended up dead."

THE DIVIDING LINE

As we read the replies, one thing stands out above all else—there is a deep dividing line between the inner city and the suburbs. Not only are these two groups not reaching out to one another, they're turning their backs on one another, and each believes he has a legitimate reason for doing so.

Survey or not, I'm convinced the wall surrounding the inner city is as real as the one that used to be in Berlin, maybe more so. Barbed wire and guns kept people from scaling that one, yet they still managed. Few, if any, have penetrated the one circling the city. It has kept two passionate people-groups separated and a whole generation of people in place. It must be built with some pretty strong bricks. If we're going to minister to those confined by it, we will have to penetrate it and do our best to tear it down. If we're to succeed as part of a spiritual demolition team, we have to discover what those bricks are made of.

NO BRICKS OF STRAW

If we take the inner-city responses and divide them up, we quickly find something.

Responses like "My people are here" and "Whitey's got me in a box" point to the same building block Audrey ran into in the park: suspicion. Those on the inside believe that no one on the outside wishes them any good. No one will allow them the freedom outside the wall that they enjoy on the inside. They suspect other things too: The police are there to suppress. The courts are there to condemn. Jobs they'd be able to get on the outside are only substandard. Education on the outside is trying to indoctrinate. Free stuff—food, clothes—is given just to convince them to drop their guard, get them to turn against their own. A tract is given just to separate them from who they truly are. Grave suspicion. And the stakes are too high to even take a chance: they might lose their identities, even their very lives.

We in the Christian community are not immune from suspicions of our own; sometimes our suspicions keep Christians inside the wall from using the tools those living outside the wall have given us.

For example, not long ago I had the opportunity to see the Christian film *Jesus,* produced by The Jesus Project. Based on the Gospel of Luke, it is an accurate depiction of Jesus' life, death, resurrection, and the gospel as a whole. I was thrilled by it and thought it would make a wonderful evangelistic tool within our neighborhood. I thought that interested members could take a copy of the film, invite friends and neighbors to see it, and after the final credits, discuss it—and Jesus. I thought it would be an excellent way of introducing our Lord and the gospel in a familiar way: video. I bought two hundred copies of the film and asked interested members to see it and use it. The reviews quickly came back. "There are no black people in this film. They've ignored us. We will not use it." It didn't matter that it was a wonderful film and a wonderful opportunity; my people were suspicious of the producer's motives and racial leanings.

This attitude is residue from another problem that plagues the inner city. Christianity is viewed by many in the black community as a white man's religion. As exemplified by the *Jesus* film, there seem to be no blacks present at the founding of Christianity, only whites—Jews, Romans, and Greeks. Of course, this simply isn't true. I'll discuss this in more length in another chapter, but for now, rest assured that black people are prominent throughout Scripture—Old and New Testaments—and in the early church as well.

But because God never mentions race, having separated the people by language, families (nations), and location, no one is overtly identified as black. Therefore in a race-conscious environment our presence and contributions are often overlooked. Even the reading of Scripture becomes a breeding ground for suspicion.

If we look at a few more of the responses, we find another building block.

ANOTHER BUILDING BLOCK

"I couldn't get a job out there" or "I couldn't afford to live out there" and "My people are here" all express fear. Of course, there's an element of fear in suspicion. We're afraid something might be true. But this building block of fear can stand on its own. People are afraid they can't make it out there, that their skill levels are so far behind that what jobs they can get won't pay the bills. And if they are lucky enough to make it, they're afraid they won't be welcomed back in the 'hood. Their success will taint them. Those who remained behind the wall would see them as having made too many compromises.

Even macho responses like "The problem's here and I'm not going to run from it" come from fear. A fear that if they do leave, they will be branded a quitter—perhaps only by themselves—but wherever the brand comes from, it burns just as hot. By staying and fighting, they take on the mantle of a hero. I'm not saying this is wrong. Social ills are only solved through internal change, but we're talking about what keeps people inside, and fear, no matter what the origin, is a powerful reason to stay put.

There's another building block.

"This ain't so bad" and "I couldn't get a job out there" and "I'd be abandoning my people" come from a defeated spirit. We're all afraid at one time or another. I remember the first time I was asked to speak at Promise Keepers, a large and growing men's outreach program; I was scared to death. I would be speaking to seventy thousand men, some good, solid Christians, some searching. If I gave a good talk, many souls might be touched, maybe some men would come to a saving

45

knowledge of our Lord Jesus. If I gave a poor talk, opportunities would be lost—maybe souls would be lost. Now I know the Lord's in control of salvation, but that didn't stop my doubts. I sweat bullets those few minutes before I stepped on stage.

The point is, I indeed stepped on stage.

I did not let fear defeat me. I overcame my fear. You've undoubtedly overcome fears of your own. I can't imagine leading a life where I didn't overcome at least one fear a day. Writing this book is absolutely terrifying.

What is very distressing is that I see my brothers and sisters in the inner city giving in to their fears, allowing their fears to govern their lives. They have succumbed to a defeated spirit.

A young lady had what I considered to be a great idea for a business. I won't tell you what it is here, but I thought if she could round up a little money, she could start something that could become quite big. Everyone with a modern office could use it. But she never started her business. Before she even began her search for capital, she stopped, sure that no one with any money would give it to a young black woman.

But what pains me more, there are many other brothers and sisters who are trying to convince those in the inner city that their fears are justified. That they can't make it on the outside; that my young black friend would indeed get the cold shoulder out there. Not because her idea was bad—which it wasn't—but because she was young, inexperienced, and, above all, black—which she was. Now she may never have raised enough capital to get her business started, but she never tried. She was defeated before she started.

Like this would-be entrepreneur, many others have been convinced that the deck is stacked so high against them, there's no way to leap over it. That while most on the outside make it just fine, those on the inside can't make it without government assistance. That their families aren't strong enough to act as a safety net.

Now there are times when our fears *are* justified. I'm deathly afraid of standing in front of a speeding train. But when it comes to facing the normal risks in life—getting a job, facing a test or life's difficulties, things that others face every day—those in the inner city are repeatedly told, and they repeatedly believe, they are ill-equipped.

When you honestly believe that you're not good enough to succeed in what others commonly do, that your intellectual and emotional faculties are less than those on the other side of the line, then you end up thinking less of yourself—you begin giving up before you start. Why put yourself through the heartache?

Other bricks may also be used to build the wall, but I'm convinced if they are, they are merely variations on these three: suspicion, fear, and a defeated spirit.

Now let's look at the wall keeping the suburbanites out of the city.

HOW THE WALL LOOKS FROM THE OUTSIDE

These responses, "I feel like an outsider" and "They probably don't want my help," give us suspicion again. Those on the outside distrust the motives of those on the inside. If they can't find a job, it's because they haven't looked hard enough. If their child's on drugs, it's because they haven't done all they could to keep him clean. If the schools are unsafe, it's because they're not being tough enough on the offenders. If the inner city wanted to clean itself up, it would. They believe problems are allowed to continue and take over. Suspicion.

Fear is an external building block too. "It's scary" or "I feel like I'm about to be attacked" are expressions of fear. These are not unfounded fears. I've mentioned people taking wrong turns and ending up dead. Such a thing happened to a couple no more than a mile from St. Stephen's. Families are innocently enjoying the night air when they are brutally gunned down. This happened to the visiting son of a brother pastor in Long Beach, California. A woman in our neighborhood was out for a morning jog and was shot and killed—a mistaken hit. Legitimate or not, fear keeps those on the outside outside.

Here is another brick in the wall. "I'm responsible for my life. They're responsible for theirs" and "I don't have to go. My money's already there—in welfare" are motivated by apathy. Large doses of it. "After all, it's their problem. What difference does it make to me?"

Now apathy isn't always a bad thing. We can't do everything. We can't even care about everything. We would go nuts. So we prioritize. Based on some sort of internal sense of what's important and what isn't, we take a look around us and make decisions about how much energy we're going to expend on things. Jumping out of the way of that speeding train probably gets a good jolt of energy, while choosing a new toothpaste gets very little. For many of us, ministering to the inner city is down there with the toothpaste. Apathy is one of the bricks in the wall.

So far I've discussed individual apathy. But there's another kind that provides its share of inaction: the apathy of the suburban churches.

The homeless problem in the inner city is staggering. I've heard statistics on the number of homeless but, frankly, they're not important. What is important is that there *are* homeless people, and when a ministry dawns and begins to help, the flow of the homeless to take advantage of it soon becomes an overwhelming flood.

Now there are some who believe the homeless could work themselves out of being homeless if they'd just put their minds and backs into it. That most, if not all, homeless people are there because in some perverted way they want to be there. People who believe this cite the numbers of jobs that go begging, or suggest if there is some kind of problem that keeps a person from getting a job—mental illness, for example—that his family should take care of him. I'm not denying any of that. In a country of 250 million, there are bound to be some who fall so far that, for whatever the reason, they are fending for themselves without jobs, homes, and most of all, hope.

What the reason is doesn't matter.

Just as we're commanded to meet people in their homes, their businesses, their places of recreation, we're also commanded to meet people on the streets. How they got there and why they stay isn't important. Prison ministries minister to murderers and thieves, child molesters and drug addicts. Why, then, because someone refuses to get a job even if he's relatively able, do we not minister to him? Is laziness worse than murder? Is an arrogant refusal to become part of the mainstream worse than thievery or drug dealing? Of course not.

So, as part of our work in the inner city, St. Stephen's set up a ministry to the homeless. In concert with other churches in the area, we distribute food, clothing, provide a place to stay at night—and, along with all that, a strong dose of the gospel. When all is said and done, Jesus' love has been shown, seeds have been planted, and some have been saved.

In a short time the demands of this ministry outstripped our meager ability to provide. I decided to ask for help. I wrote letters to fifty suburban churches in the San Diego area, each much more affluent than our own. I explained in detail what we were doing and the results we were having. I asked the leadership at those churches for assistance that we might represent them in this endeavor. Only one of those fifty churches even replied, and although we were thankful for their gift, it was no more than a token of what is needed.

Those ministering on the green hills and mountains can often lose sight of the battle raging on the parched plains below.

They are mired in apathy—perhaps that same apathy that keeps one on the streets. In any case, it's the apathy that keeps them from even trying to cross the line surrounding our inner cities.

WHO BUILT THE WALL?

Satan drew the line around the inner city. He's the one who built the wall.

And the mortar he uses to fuse the bricks together is his lies.

A friend's son was getting ready to go to college. He had done reasonably well in high school, and with affirmative action programs he was admitted to one of the more prestigious colleges in the state. I heard about it and gave him the names of some local churches and contacts at Campus Crusade. I thought the experience would be good for the young man.

The instant his friends heard about it, they began to work on him. "You don't want to go there. Stay around here—with your people. Nobody wants you there. Anyway, you'll never make it. Whitey's going to make your life miserable. The teachers will flunk you. And if you make it, all that means is you've become one of them."

He didn't go.

The lie wasn't that he might meet those kinds of obstacles. We all know that racism still exists in our country. The lie was that he would be stopped by it. That he didn't have the courage to hit the wall, bounce back, then smash through it the next time. That he was emotionally and spiritually weak.

Satan worked on him through his "friends."

Satan is called the "father of all lies." And he's lying to us, in this case feeding that boy's suspicions, fears, and his defeated spirit.

Another friend who lives outside the city was thinking about finding a corner in the inner city and passing out tracts in broad daylight. He wasn't planning on preaching; in fact, he wasn't planning on saying much of anything at all. He was just going to find a relatively busy spot and start handing out the gospel.

He went looking for the right corner. Taking a half-day vacation from work, he headed toward the city. The lies started buzzing in his head the instant he neared what he thought would be the turnoff. "If you get lost, you're dead. And what if it's a corner used by some drug dealer? He's not going to react kindly to this intrusion."

He could actually feel his blood pressure rise.

But he knew that God had not given him a soul of timidity. And even if he had, God was right there in the car with him. He took the turnoff and headed into the city.

Now the buzzing became even more insistent.

"This is a pretty rough place. Wouldn't you think God would have sent someone a little better prepared to deal with it? Someone with a little more experience? What if you have to cut and run real fast? You don't even jog. There's no way you could outrun a bullet. Do you have any idea how much you don't belong here?"

There was a corner. By a strip mall with a chain drugstore in it. Reasonably busy. He could stand right there by the bus stop and hand out the gospel tracts.

"Look at the store on the end of the strip mall; it's burned out. There was probably a riot here the last time some guy showed up to hand out tracts."

When the man gave in to the buzzing and got back home he felt so relieved that he'd survived, he decided he would just write a donation check to a small church he'd seen not far from that corner and suggest they pass out tracts themselves.

Satan is whispering lies in our mind's ear. As he did with the college-bound lad, he fed my friend's suspicions about the area and pushed him back into his box of inaction, showing him that his apathy was right.

Now, please understand, I'm not advocating people overcome the lies and leave the inner city. Quite the contrary. I believe the inner city's salvation comes when people stay, come to a saving knowledge of Jesus, and begin living godly lives. As people are saved, the inner city will change, burned and ravaged neighborhoods will transform themselves into God's garden as the gospel blooms there. And if I know God at all, the garden will be more beautiful than we could ever imagine.

But even though we know how wonderful it would be if God brought revival to the inner city, why should we work at becoming part of it? What if revival isn't his plan? What if, like on so many mission fields, the workers slog it out one soul at a time?

But whether there is revival or a long, difficult row to hoe, we still have to minister to those living there. We've talked a little about the line surrounding the inner city and the fear, suspicion, and defeated spirits that keep people there. Now let's talk about the foundation of that wall, the stuff that feeds those bricks and keeps them strong.

Let's talk about the rage.

CHAPTER 4

Racism, Rage, AND REBELLION

Then . . . God relented from the disaster that He had said He would bring upon them, and He did not do it. But it displeased Jonah exceedingly, and he became angry.

Jonah 3:10–4:1

At the base of Jonah's rebellion was rage. Anger that the God about and for whom he prophesied, the God he trusted and prayed to, was about to give his enemy the opportunity for salvation. He wanted no part of it. And, since Jonah was an Israelite, it's easy to understand his point of view.

Nineveh was the capital of Assyria. Assyria's heart. Its head. In Scripture Assyria is called cruel, destructive, selfish, unfaithful, proud, and haughty in its dealings with Israel. In 2 Kings Assyria is said to have ravaged Israel and reduced her to tribute. Assyria had insulted and threatened Judah, before invading Israel again. Assyria blasphemed the Lord. So Assyria was no ordinary enemy. This was an enemy committed to Israel's annihilation, a hateful, deceitful enemy without an ounce of honor. A rattlesnake of an enemy.

And God wanted to give this enemy one more chance!

"How could you, Lord?"

How many Israelites had Jonah seen slaughtered? How many Israelites' lives had been disrupted? You can almost hear Jonah complaining. "Aren't *you* our Lord? Haven't we sacrificed for *you*—to *you*—worked for *you*—praised *your* name? *You're* my God. Mine. And you're ministering to my *enemy*?" Jonah hated the Ninevites. A deep and personal hatred.

And that was probably why the Lord wanted to use Jonah for this mission.

For the same reason that the rich young ruler of the New Testament was asked to give up all his wealth and follow Jesus, Jonah was asked to bring the "repent now" message to Nineveh.

In the last chapter we discussed the bricks used to build the wall that imprisons the inner city. Now let's talk about that wall's foundation. This foundation not only supports the wall, feeds the bricks, and gives them strength, but it also goes down deep, making digging it out or burrowing under it quite difficult. What is the foundation made of? Rage.

But this isn't just ordinary rage.

The story I'm going to tell now delves deeply into the personal life of a dear friend. It's all true. Some may think it sounds a little like a psychological *Star Trek* episode in that it discusses things that reside deeply within him—his inner space, his inner "black holes"—and includes reasons for behavior that are seen only by him and interpreted by his therapist.

A SPECIAL KIND OF RAGE

My friend Ted is white. He was raised in an alcoholic home. Ted's father, who had been drinking since he was a teen, had grown up without a father; he died early from wounds suffered during World War I. Ted's mother was too busy dealing with his dad to be an involved parent. So there was little encouragement, even less support, and a lot of criticism. Ted grew up believing he was alone in this life—afraid, living only for today, feeling inadequate to any task, and generally inadequate as a human being. A feeling Ted tried to mask by being as perfect as possible—or at least presenting himself as perfect so people couldn't see his real self.

When he was a child, his parents often played emotionally charged psychological games with each other—and he was invariably their pawn.

And, like any pawn, Ted's needs were consistently subverted to the needs of the players. When they weren't playing, Ted was largely ignored. As an adult, when his first marriage failed, the severe emotional bruises caused him to seek psychological counseling—lovingly called therapy—which he continued off and on for the next twenty-three years.

After eighteen years in counseling, he was able to determine that the truth about his conflicted emotions lay deep within himself, buried by layer upon layer of scar tissue produced by lies he had always told himself. "I have to be perfect." "I am not loved." "I am alone." "I have to make it on my own." "I'm incapable of loving." Although Ted knew little else at that point, he did know that they were lies. And he also knew that the lies were instinctive. They bubbled up from somewhere below, like an acidic subterranean spring, and when the bubbles burst on the surface, they turned his sense of well-being into a sea of dread. He also knew that to "reprogram" himself would take a lot of work—a lot of digging—and courage, for he had no idea what he would find feeding that spring. He also sensed there was no one, certainly not any of the counselors so far, who was able to do that kind of digging with him.

"Coincidentally," at that moment one came along.

Because Ted's second marriage was beginning to show severe strain, he went looking for a new counselor. A friend suggested her brother-in-law, a Christian counselor. At their first session Ted knew he had found someone who wanted to work as hard as he did to uncover whatever was there to uncover.

Ted was now in his late forties. He loved the Lord but couldn't imagine the Lord loved him, and since the Lord didn't love him—who else could? According to his counselor, denying the Lord's love was the real sin.

For a couple of years they worked to identify the source of those feelings of inadequacy, of being defeated before he'd begun. Two things emerged. One, he did not dare be himself, because he believed he was so despicable that if he was himself, everyone close to him would desert him. At a surface level, he was angry at his parents for creating such tension inside him. And that was number two: the anger. This was no ordinary anger. This anger was so great, he believed that if it got loose the world could not contain it—and he would be crushed under the weight of it. Both notions were themselves imaginary, but both involuntarily governed his behavior.

In the counselor's eyes, the anger, or rage, was foundational to most, if not all, the feelings. They concentrated on it. First, when did it start? How long had the rage been growing? The answer came in a curious, though graphic, way.

One evening while driving home, Ted had a breakthrough—what could only be called a vision. Almost involuntarily he found himself looking deeply within. There he saw what he described as a large "pod." It lay there somewhere inside, within an unfathomably dark void. He was looking at his rage; he knew it instinctively. A rock-hard meteor of a rage, a fist. As he "watched," the pod opened, separating top from bottom. After a moment he saw inside. Cradled there was a baby. Also instinctively he knew it was himself as a baby.

"That's when you started hiding inside your anger," his counselor interpreted. "Your anger is a powerful thing. You've been hiding there within it, using it to protect you, since you were a baby."

Reliving the vision several times, Ted came to the conclusion that the baby was the *real* him, a "him" he'd tucked away so the world would only see the "him" he wanted the world to see—the *perfect* him.

But how could such a rage start that young?

Babies get angry—any mother knows that, and knows when. The cry is more insistent, the face more agitated, the hands shudder and wag like tight rubber. We've all seen that in babies. Their anger is a demand for change—a demand that whatever is making them uncomfortable end. Babies get hungry, uncomfortable, even hurt, and they have no ability to change things themselves. Naturally, they make demands of others. But when the changes consistently do not occur, when their demands are seldom, if ever, met, even babies will accumulate their anger. And this anger, like drops filling a reservoir, gets bigger as time and the emotional bruises mount.

Ted once heard a story about something that happened when he was a baby. One night, when he was about nine months old, his parents neglected to feed him because they were embroiled in a power play over *who* would feed him. He had remained hungry until nearly midnight. It was the same power play he and his sister would later engage in when it came time to feed the family dog.

God tells us that we are created in his image. Although we're not God, we were created in many ways to be *like* God. He is creative; we are creative. He thinks; we think. He loves; we love. He wants justice; we want justice. And so forth. But what might be our greatest similarity? What did he name himself at the burning bush? *I am.* We often call him *The Great I Am.* He is telling us that HE IS. He exists. He is worthy. He has value, by his very nature. Of course, when you are speaking of God you're talking about the ultimate value—the ultimate worthiness—the ultimate existence.

Well, we exist too. And although we are less worthy than God, we still believe ourselves worthy. Although we are less valuable than God, we still believe ourselves to have value. In fact, we believe we have value by our very nature. We deserve to be considered—our feelings, our thoughts, our talents, our beliefs—all parts that make us *us* deserve to be thought of as having value. Some may be of greater or lesser value depending on circumstances, but none should be dismissed outright. When they are, we are diminished—our worth is attacked and the injustice of it stokes our anger.

How angry do *you* feel when you are treated contemptuously? As if you have no value? Ignored? Worse than ignored, ridiculed?

Just as God gets angry when other gods are put before him, we get angry when other people, other things, are consistently placed before us by those who should be doing just the opposite—mothers, fathers, friends, society.

All of his life his parents had discounted Ted's value as a son and as a man. One event at a time. Often little events, sometimes big events. But each told him he was insignificant, that what he thought didn't matter, that what he wanted wasn't important, and those events added up like water drops draining into a reservoir held back by a dam that never opened. Or when it did—when the ducts were opened and the rage spewed out on whomever or whatever had provoked him—he would close it up again as quickly as he was emotionally able. As time went on the reservoir of rage got broader and deeper.

The energy it took to keep that reservoir under control and bottled up was enormous. It siphoned energy away from everything else—his work, his relationships, his hopes, and his God. Because Ted felt so irrelevant, he worked at only those things that made him feel relevant—he worked for God. Not because he loved God, but because such work was relevant work and if he didn't, God would punish him—because he didn't deserve to be loved. After all, he was without worth.

Since he was in his late forties, that reservoir of rage had grown into a formidable force. And the more the counselor and Ted worked to drain it, the nearer it seemed to get to the surface. But each time my friend came close to smashing that dam and letting the rage drain away, usually during one of the counseling sessions when he reduced himself to tears, he would withdraw from the dam—swallowing the rage again.

For if he didn't withdraw, if the rage broke loose, nothing was big enough to hold it. Ted fantasized about being in the desert, hundred of miles from any people, where he could begin screaming—just screaming and screaming and screaming—until his screams sucked the reservoir dry, spewing the rage into . . . and that was the problem. Into what? The desert wasn't big enough to contain it, the universe wasn't, heaven wasn't, neither was the God who reigned there.

When he told the therapist of his fantasy, the focus of his counseling changed. God *is* big enough to absorb the rage, absorb it and still love him afterward. My friend was convinced intellectually, but not psychologically.

Now boiling just below the surface, the rage dampened every aspect of his life even more. He treated his wife abruptly and without compassion. He couldn't stand to be in the same room with his mother for more than fifteen minutes without wanting to strangle her. He couldn't speak to his father at all. Worse, though, was his relationship with God. It was formal, dispassionate, and based on a need for his own perfection— it was the relationship of a slave to a cruel master.

Then came Promise Keepers, the men's outreach program. Ted attended one of the stadium meetings. About ten o'clock on a Saturday morning, the hot L.A. sun beating down on them, sixty thousand men sang a song that asked Jesus to come closer to them. As he sang, my friend saw, almost physically, his anger standing in the way of Jesus coming nearer. Since he had been praying for years for the anger to be removed, he saw no use in praying again. Unable to sing for the tears, Ted thrust longing hands into the air and lamented how Jesus would always be distant from him, that he would never experience the fellowship he longed for.

For the first time Ted truly understood the wedge his rage had placed between him and the Lord. But the Lord performed a miracle of grace in Ted's life. Suddenly, as if by magic—"now the burden's there, now it's not"—my friend sensed the rage had vanished, completely removed from his heart like an excised tumor. He felt happy, released; he felt true joy. A smile spread across his face like sunlight breaking from a cloud. And Jesus was right there—in his heart, in his mind—intimately a part of him. Nothing stood between them anymore.

Not long thereafter was Mother's Day and he took his mother out for a long Sunday brunch. He began speaking to his father again. And although these relationships are not perfect, they are at least ongoing.

More happened. Ted had always been contemptuous of his fellow human beings, and if compassion was due one of them, he would have to consciously manufacture it. Now compassion came naturally. And he was shocked at its depth. A stranger spoke of losing her son to a murderer. Before he would have had to search for words of sympathy, now he actually wept openly.

And there was another change.

Before that Promise Keepers moment, his home, office, and car were a mess. Belongings stacked everywhere. He never put anything away. He never took the time. He was always too busy running to per-fection to stop and maintain anything. When the anger evaporated, all that changed. Ted starting spending hours on Saturday mornings cleaning. Before, he had a cleaning lady that came in every two weeks. He let her go. He didn't need her anymore. Ted deserves to live in a neater, more eye-pleasing place, and he's now willing to take the time to make it so.

I asked my friend if I could use his story of emo-tional redemption because it parallels the black per-son's path to rage in many ways.

But before we begin, I need to say something. I'm going to discuss racism and how it causes black Amer-icans to be angry, much like Ted was angry. At times it will seem like I'm pointing a finger at those read-ing this as the source of that racism. I'm not. We are Christians, and if we have the Spirit of God working within us, although we may have lapses—on both sides of the racial divide—they are only lapses. We love each other and race has no place in our affections for God and his people. Also, as Christians, if we are sinned against, our response is clear: love in return.

But racism exists in this country, indeed in just about every country. What follows will give you an idea of how deep it goes.

BLACK RAGE

A nine-year-old white boy loved his father, a real man's man. Dad took him hunting, fishing, played catch with him, taught him the way to hold a bat and swing it so all the power was right there in the thick of the wood. They would often go for long walks in the woods, or stand by the fishing pond skipping rocks while they talked—sometimes about nothing, sometimes about important things.

One day the father decided it was time to tell his son about black people. The nine year old is a man now and doesn't remember every word that was said, but this white father was telling his boy how blacks were less able to do things than whites. Blacks couldn't fix cars as well, couldn't fish as well, so the boy was to watch out for black folks. "Don't stake too much on them—don't give them your car to fix or nothing like that."

His father couldn't do anything mechanical. His mother fixed everything around the house, but, of course, no one ever said anything about that. So taking his car to someone he trusted was important. Knowing this, but not knowing the sensitivities, the boy made a joke. "I guess no black guy could ever fix a car as good as you do." He laughed, expecting his father to laugh with him. He didn't. He only stared at the boy for what seemed like forever—an angry stare—one you might give someone you love who'd just stabbed you right in the heart.

The man never had a conversation with his boy again. He would tell him to take out the trash and clean up his room, but those long, loving conversations were a thing of the past. "Equate me with a black man and there's no second chance. No matter who you are."

THE STEADY HUMILIATION

That story illustrates the deeply held prejudice that has resulted in the steady humiliation of an entire race.

A black man on a rural construction project is always the one chosen to move the outhouse—to cover the "filled" hole and dig the new one.

A black waitress at a truck stop frequented mostly by white drivers is treated well but tipped only half what others get.

A black man with a wife and two kids is fired from his job at an auto wrecking yard for stealing and reselling auto parts—something he didn't do. He later finds out the guy who fired him had been selling the parts under the table and needed a fall guy for an IRS audit. He also learned that he was chosen rather than two Hispanic kids who worked there because the accusation would be easily believed.

A black man takes his wife to a fine restaurant for their anniversary. A member of the upper middle class, he drives a Buick for family use and a Porsche for fun. He dresses impeccably and is a refined member of the community in every way. But even though, by any measure, he belongs at that restaurant, the white busboy refuses to serve him water, walking repeatedly by his table while serving the other guests. When the black man complains, the maître d' reprimands the busboy in the back, but the young man still refuses to serve the black man and is simply assigned another table. Another busboy brings what my friend requires. What if a black busboy had refused to serve a white guest?

A black man reads about a government experiment. Some blacks who had contracted syphilis were allowed to die untreated just so other men, both white and black, could see how the disease progressed in men of color. Is a presidential apology enough? Shouldn't someone be punished? Or were his black brothers really just two-legged lab rats?

A made-for-television miniseries about black tribes in Africa freely reveals black women's breasts. The reason this is allowed on television is that it's factual—that's the way they dressed—and it's daring. But would white, brown, or yellow women's breasts be shown like that?

And, as with Ted, rage can start at an early age. A six-year-old black boy is asked to a birthday party in a predominantly white neighborhood. The main attraction at the party is a pony ride. The white operator of the ride says the black boy is too small to ride, although he gives smaller white boys a turn. Only after a parent complains is the black boy allowed on the pony but then under the hateful gaze of the operator.

Chipping away, a blow at a time. A steady, long-term attack on a black person's value as a human being. Incident after incident. Each reaffirming that the black person is of less worth. The rage mounts, the reservoir deepens.

For Rent signs that come down as a black couple approach.

Raises withheld.

Jobs denied.

Seats on crowded buses blocked off by packages when a black person eyes them.

White men who force their attentions on black women because they just naturally assume they're of a lower moral character.

The stress against the dam is huge.

It would not be quite so bad if a person's anger were based only on what he or she personally experienced. But it's not. Parents make an early deposit into those reservoirs. They were angry too, the result of the emotional battering they and their parents had to endure. The blatant racism: white hoods and burning crosses, the segregation, the denial of services basic to normal life, the substandard medical attention, the paupers' graves. The institutionalized racism: the separate schools, the black drinking fountains, the back of the bus, the denial of the vote, the injustice in the courts and in the military. The violence, the rapes, the murders—and the lynchings.

Generations of racism have left deep, deep scars on the soul of the black community. These wounds are not easily healed, as the following story illustrates.

> The Negro man of eighty told a story. He was twelve and a playmate was tied in a cage waiting to be taken away and lynched. The shackled boy stood accused of raping a white woman.
>
> The old man recalled the fright which caused him to run away the next day. From that time on he never knew a home. His years were spent roaming about the country. He became an itinerant preacher, forever invoking God, but always too terrified to return to his place of birth. When asked why, he would reply: "The white folks down there are too mean."
>
> For most of this life he was tortured by memories. Every place he stopped, he soon became frightened and moved on. Sometimes in the middle of a sermon he would cry out: "How could they do that to a boy?" (From *Black Rage*, William H. Grier and Price M. Cobbs, BasicBooks, 1968, p. 27)

Now imagine you are the parent of the boy who was lynched. An angry parent will produce an angry child.

The anger may be justified, but haven't white Americans apologized, made sincere attempts to make things right? Are what black people see as racial incidents merely the acts of the insensitive or the "jerks" of our society? My white friends complain about those same "jerks."

But it doesn't matter how much is real or how much is imagined. We are called to meet people where they are, and if their behavior and view of the world are governed in any way by that rage, we need to learn to deal with it.

For, just as it was with Ted, there is no constructive way for those suffering from it to easily and effectively release it.

Society in general doesn't recognize it as legitimate, and expressing it within the black community doesn't help much either. If anything, the rage increases. Get in a small group and start expressing the anger and one expression produces another, and soon each person's rage has fed on the others and been multiplied in intensity by the number of people taking part.

Racism is teaching young black men and women that they truly aren't as good as their white counterparts. Welfare tells them they can't feed their families without help, while white men and women can. Not only is their rage growing because of that assault, it's growing because frequently the generally accepted leadership is continually telling them that the white man is keeping them down and they're not strong enough to overcome the hurdles.

So, when you blend governmental racial discrimination with the negative message ringing from many of today's leadership, black and white, then throw in the true racism that still exists in this country, which stands atop racism throughout history—you end up with a very deep, very broad reservoir of rage seething in the guts of most black people today.

And sometimes it can actually be seen—when it explodes to the surface.

A video on the evening news showed a black man upset because he had been ticketed for parking at an expired meter. He got there just after the ticket was placed under the windshield wiper, and, of course, the traffic cop, a smallish Latino man, wouldn't tear it up. We've all been in similar situations. Maybe not with parking meters, but perhaps with a store that puts up the closed sign the moment our hand hits the door. Normally we just make a quick request (maybe a demand), are refused, and go on.

In this case the confrontation was on. It was a frightening thing to watch. The black man, in much better shape than the officer, ranted and raved, flailed his arms as if to threaten him bodily, and for a moment looked like he might actually attack the much smaller man. It only ended when the black man's ire turned to a general frustration and defeat. He threw up his hands, uttered a profanity or two, and stalked off. Much angrier than that particular situation warranted, the black man was probably thinking that the system whitey had created had won again.

Such rage explodes even at church. At one time I had a black staff member who was married to a white woman. They had two wonderful children and seemed very much in love, certainly in love enough to withstand the prejudice against mixed marriages that exists on both sides. One evening the family sat down in front of the television to watch Alex Haley's *Roots*. Suddenly the man was overcome with anger. It seemed all the injustice blacks had been forced to endure—all the disrespect he'd gotten throughout his life—was suddenly focused on the white woman sitting there in the room with him. Later he told me he felt like beating her. The rage never resubmerged. It seemed to take over his life. He and his wife were subsequently divorced, and I've since lost track of them.

As with my friend Ted, black rage colors every aspect of black life. It saps the energy, explodes without warning, causes people to do things they wouldn't ordinarily do. And it causes them to behave differently toward a white person than they normally would. They might be subdued, or overly aggressive, perhaps evade the eyes, speak in short sentences, and try desperately to get away.

Of course, everybody is different. Some are more or less angry, some are more able to suppress the symptoms of the anger than others. But I dare say that every black man you will encounter to some extent or another has that reservoir of rage boiling inside him.

This is not to excuse any rudeness you might encounter. But it is to explain *what* you may encounter.

AT THE FOOT OF THE CROSS

The other reason I wanted to tell Ted's story is to point out the Lord's mercy with him. After years of hard work he was still unable to drain that sea of anger. The only way it left was through what my friend legitimately calls a miracle of God's grace.

A miracle that many of my black brothers and sisters have already experienced through the saving mercies of our Lord Jesus Christ. Oh, what a grand moment that is when we look out over the world of faces and see the love of Jesus shining there—the hate and the anger gone. But like my dear friend who found his rage while watching *Roots*, some people do not automatically empty that reservoir of anger at salvation. Sometimes a new Christian simply tries to bury it deeper, and the anger only leaves, if it ever does, when the brother or sister lays it at the foot of the cross.

I've expended so many words on this subject because it's important to understand that whether you think it's justified or not, the rage is there. And, though directed your way at the moment, it isn't personal. Nor is it something that the person can easily brush away. Usually, however, you'll never see it exposed. Like Ted, the person is schooled at suppressing it. But if you minister to the inner city and begin to discuss the deeper things of life with the people you find there, you may touch a nerve or two. When you do, it might be a little frightening for you. But that's good. It shows the person is listening, thinking, allowing your message to touch the emotions, perhaps the soul. *You are piercing the wall. Crossing the line.*

Also be aware that when you do see it firsthand, the best approach to dealing with it is love. Not a syrupy, condescending, "oh, poor guy" kind of love. But a love born in respect for who this person is. Born in the realization that he or she has value before God, and his or her life and struggle, just like yours, have meaning and importance—that he or she *personally* has meaning and importance.

RAGING AT GOD

There is another thing to recognize: ultimately, black rage, indeed most rage, is focused on God. The prayer inevitably is: *God, why have you put me through this?* If God wanted the black person's life to be better, it would be. And the black person knows this. Although he'll say he's angry at whitey, he's really mad at God.

This is actually a value in ministry.

That's why Ted saw the rage as separating God and himself; it was because his rage was ultimately at God. God had given him those parents. God was supposed to take care of him as a baby, a teen, or an adult, and he hadn't—at least not in the way Ted thought he should. Ted was mad at God. Even so, God not only absorbed it, but in the twinkling of an eye, he dissolved it.

When our black brothers and sisters begin to identify it, they will also believe their rage is huge, perhaps too huge to be dealt with. It's a great comfort to tell them that even though they may be angry at God, he is big enough to absorb the shock of it. And his grace is big enough to cover it.

A COLOR-BLIND FAITH

We've talked about the bricks that make up the wall—
fear, suspicion, and a defeated spirit. We've expanded
on that to discuss the foundation of rage, which feeds
those bricks and keeps them strong and resistant to
penetration.

Next we're going to confront the notion that Christianity is a white man's religion.

Is it? Are we trying to force something on people
of color that they have a right to mistrust? Or has God
included people of color in Scripture and in the early
church, making Christianity a faith all people can
embrace?

CHAPTER 5

The Heritage of the BLACK CHRISTIAN

You have brought up my life from the pit, O Lord, my God.

Jonah 2:6

Did you know Moses married a black woman? Or that the first king mentioned in the Bible was also black? Or that a black man carried the cross for our Lord and Savior Jesus Christ? Or that three early popes were black?

Growing up, I didn't, and even today many of my black brothers and white brothers don't either. Is it important? Not to the Lord, and we'll discuss why in a second, but it is important to the inner city and our evangelistic efforts there.

A WHITE MAN'S RELIGION

As I mentioned, there is a suspicion of Christianity within the black community. Some label it a "white man's religion"—after all, except for the black leaders today, there doesn't seem to be much evidence that black people had much to do with Christianity's formation or its early growth. White Europeans seem to have just thought it up, brought it over here, and are now trying to build their numbers and treasure by appealing to blacks.

And it also appears that those black people who become a part of it suddenly start embracing whites, which neutralizes their effectiveness in the ongoing black struggle. A double whammy.

As a result, many blacks stay away from the Christian church, either remaining a part of the secular world or joining black-oriented religions—the Black Muslims, for example.

When you read the Bible, that actually seems like a reasonable position to take. Seldom is anyone identified as black, particularly any leaders of the early Christian movement. However, when you take a closer look you find that many in Scripture *are* black and they show up, just as whites do, on both sides of salvation's fence.

I realize that the inner city is populated by all races, but this issue seems to be a stumbling block for many of our black brothers. So, let's take a moment and examine it, not only for my black brothers and sisters who suffer from this misconception, but also for my white brothers and sisters, who might also benefit from some light shed on this area.

America is foundationally a white, European country. Yet blacks were involved in significant ways before the Mayflower ever landed. Regrettably their contributions have been largely ignored or left out of history and literature. There's nothing wrong with that. It's just fact. Those people who have shaped this country historically were predominantly white Europeans.

When books or newspapers are written, unless otherwise stated, the characters are assumed to be white. It was assumed from the opening words that Scarlett O'Hara was white, or Perry Mason, or any other character you can name.

Because of this, however, when we read the Bible we apply the same standard. The difference is that the Lord seldom identifies people by race. Not that race isn't important to him, it's just not one of the ways he's chosen to separate people. We're told about the survivors of the great Flood in Genesis—Noah, Shem, Ham, and Japheth, and their wives—and how they repopulated the world. The Lord, through Moses, tells us that "from these the coastland peoples . . . were separated into their lands, everyone according to his language, according to their families, into their nations" (Gen. 10:5).

God never intended us to be separated by race. And why should he have? If we look at that first surviving family, those eight members of it, every race that now exists was within their DNA and resulting genes. In fact, there probably would have been no separation at all, except that which would have occurred naturally as members of that original family grew in numbers and sought land on which to support themselves, if some people had not rebelled against God by erecting the Tower of Babel. In order to thwart man's determination to thwart God, he separated us by language so we could not communicate.

But if God did not separate by race, we should see black people throughout Scripture.

And that's what we see.

In Genesis 10:6 we read, "The sons of Ham were Cush, Mizraim, Put, and Canaan." Cush means *black*.

Names in Israel meant something. It doesn't take much of an imagination to put yourself in Ham's place. His first son, the son who would inherit most of his wealth, was dark-skinned. He named him Cush. At this point there were probably fewer than twenty people living on earth; this is the postflood origin of the black race. Since we now have a starting point, we can begin to identify some of the people of color in Scripture.

But before we start, let me say something else. Since the Lord saw fit not to separate his people by race, I run the risk of offending him by doing so here. As you will see as we identify those in Scripture who were almost certainly people of color, the Lord wanted the races to live together not only as neighbors but as family. My intent, therefore, is to show both my black and my white brothers and sisters that Christianity is, in a very real and practical sense, color-blind.

A BEGINNING

Nimrod, "a mighty hunter before the Lord," was the first warrior-king on earth, the first builder of an empire. Identified as a descendant of Cush, he was, therefore, almost certainly a black man.

Moving forward in time we come to Joseph, Jacob's son and one of the twelve Israelite patriarchs. Joseph's brothers, jealous over their father's special relationship with him, sold him into slavery, which eventually brought him to Egypt. Joseph showed Pharaoh that he had a special relationship with the Lord God by interpreting a dream that saved Egypt from severe famine. After that, the Bible tells us, "Pharaoh called

Joseph's name Zaphnath-Paaneah. And he gave him as a wife Asenath, the daughter of Poti-Pherah priest of On. So Joseph went out over all the land of Egypt" (Gen. 41:45).

Tracing Asenath's genealogy, we find that she was of the Hamitic line through Cush. She is believed to be a black woman, the Hamitic line being in power at that time. Since Joseph was then a resident of Egypt, it is even more likely that the wife Pharaoh gave to Joseph was a black woman. Genesis 41:50 says: "And to Joseph were born two sons before the years of famine came, whom Asenath, the daughter of Poti-Pherah priest of On, bore to him." That would make the two sons, Ephraim and Manasseh, men of color—thus making them an interracial family, a blending of the blood of Shem and the blood of Ham.

When we come to the life of Moses, we read, "Then Miriam and Aaron spoke against Moses because of the Ethiopian [Cushite] woman whom he had married; for he had married an Ethiopian [Cushite] woman" (Num. 12:1). God wants us to make no mistake here: he calls the descendants of Cush either Cushites or Ethiopians. Ethiopian meant "burned-up face, dark face, the black face"—in other words, black people, ebony people. Moses married a black woman named Zipporah.

As we see from Miriam's and Aaron's reactions, there was prejudice against interracial marriage even in those days—but it was not a prejudice shared by God, who struck Miriam with leprosy because of her prejudice (Num. 12:10). For not only did he have Moses marry a black woman, but he also placed Zipporah's father, Jethro, in the priesthood of the Midianites—a group traced back through the lineage of Cush.

Then, as if to put an exclamation point on this interracial blending, we see that Moses asks his brother-in-law, Hobab, to help the Israelites. "Please do not leave, inasmuch as you know how we are to camp in the wilderness, and you can be our eyes" (Num. 10:31). Hobab took a position as part of Israel's leadership. He led Moses and the people of God in at least part of their wilderness experience.

Now we come to Solomon and his powerful love poem, Song of Solomon. Solomon, the probable subject of the poem, was of the line of Shem; his wife and lover was of the line of Cush.

In Solomon's poem she says, "Let him kiss me with the kisses of his mouth— / For your love is better than wine. / Because of the fragrance of your good ointments, / Your name is ointment poured forth" (1:2–3). It goes on: "The king has brought me into his chambers. / We will be glad and rejoice in you. / We will remember your love more than wine. / Rightly do they love you" (1:4).

Then we come to verse 5: "I am dark, but lovely, / O daughters of Jerusalem." (In the King James Version it reads, "I am black, but comely.") Verse 6 says, "Do not look upon me, because I am dark." Some versions use *black* or *swarthy* in translating this verse.

Whichever word you use, the wife of Solomon is reiterating, "I am black."

The Queen of Sheba is also in the roster of black biblical characters. Sheba was the son of Raamah, son of Cush, and this woman was the queen of that group of people descended from Cush through Raamah.

Even biblical historians like Josephus, Origen, and Jerome confirm she was a black woman. She is mentioned quite prominently and respectfully as a woman eager to learn Solomon's wisdom, the implication being that she wanted to bring what she would learn back to her people.

Zephaniah, a prophet in the time of Josiah, was also probably black. He was the son of Cushi (a variant of Cush or a Cushite), meaning black.

THE NEW TESTAMENT

Are people of color represented in the New Testament?

Let's look at the early church, as described in the book of Acts. The author tells us: "Now in the church that was at Antioch there were certain prophets and teachers: Barnabas, Simeon who was called Niger, Lucius of Cyrene . . ." (13:1).

Niger is Latin for *black*. A derivative of the term was borrowed from the Spanish and Portuguese and became *Negro*, a word that has fallen to disfavor among most black people.

So, there were black prophets and teachers in the New Testament church. As if to confirm this, the next person on the list of church leaders at Antioch was Lucius of Cyrene. Cyrene was in North Africa, in the region known today as Libya. Although not specifically mentioned, there is a good chance that Lucius was also black.

Remember Simon of Cyrene? As the angry mob led Jesus away after they had falsely judged him, beaten him, mocked him, and placed a bloodletting thorny crown upon his head, he undoubtedly stumbled while carrying his cross. A Roman soldier pulled Simon of Cyrene from the crowd to shoulder that cross the rest of the way to Golgotha—the Place of the Skull—the site of our Lord's crucifixion. We know where Cyrene is and what Simon probably was.

Now there are those who use this illustration to further the notion that the black man is meant to carry the white man's burden. Can you actually believe that's what Jesus would think of this man? No. Simon was there as an illustration for all of us as followers of Christ. In this illustration a man, who was probably black, was a model for all believers—he was Everyman. As believers we are equals—black, white, brown, yellow, red. Color is in man's eyes, not God's.

Did a black man appear in Scripture after the Lord's resurrection?

I direct you again to the book of Acts: "Now an angel of the Lord spoke to Philip, saying, 'Arise and go toward the south along the road which goes down from Jerusalem to Gaza.' This is desert. So he arose and went. And behold, a man of Ethiopia, a eunuch of great authority under Candace the queen of the Ethiopians, who had charge of all her treasury, and had come to Jerusalem to worship, was returning" (8:26–28).

An angel told Philip where to find this Ethiopian official; Philip led him to salvation and baptized him in a stream nearby. Now why was this Ethiopian, this black man, saved in such a miraculous way? When he returned to Ethiopia, this man planted the seed of the church that would one day be called Abyssinian. Historically, the Abyssinian church of Ethiopia was associated with the Coptic church of Egypt—an affiliation that still exists. These churches, rooted in North Africa, have branches in the United States today.

The early church was also guided by prominent black men. Three Catholic popes were black: Victor the First (A.D. 189–199), who was martyred for the faith; Melchiades, also known as Miltiades (A.D. 311–314); and Gelasius (A.D. 492–496). All were canonized by the Catholic church as saints.

Another prominent black man was one of the greatest of the early church leaders, Saint Augustine.

He was born in A.D. 354 in Algeria. His mother, Monica, was a devout Christian. His father, Patricius, was a pagan who came from a formerly wealthy family of landowners. Augustine lived during the decline of the Roman Empire and held the position of Bishop of Hippo in North Africa for thirty-five years. Saint Ambrose probably baptized him in Milan, Italy, in A.D. 386.

Saint Augustine wrote two influential books; his first, *Confessions*, was a vivid account of his early life and religious development. In it he speaks boldly of his repentance from sin and how his sins had troubled him. He wrote his second, *The City of God*, to restore confidence in the Christian church as Rome was disintegrating. In the Middle Ages those who argued that the church was above the state—that God's law is above man's—used this book as a proof text. His other writings on communal life form what is called the *Rule of St. Augustine*, which is the basis for many religious orders. A man of great influence and intellect: a man of color. (More proof of Saint Augustine, and other early Christians, being a man of color can be found in the book *Impact of the African Tradition on African*

Christianity by Nya Kwiawon Taryor Sr., Strugglers' Community Press.)

In this brief chapter we've shown that black men and women have been active not only in the foundations of the Christian church, but also in its leadership. The Christian faith is not a white man's religion, it is a way of salvation for all men and women, regardless of race. God calls his people from everywhere to himself. Our job, then, is to carry the gospel to all, so that God's people may hear it and respond to it.

I cannot end this chapter without acknowledging where most of my information here was gleaned. I am deeply indebted to my brothers in the faith, Luther Blackwell and Walter McCray. Both have done extensive research into this area, and I recommend their books: Blackwell's *The Heritage of the Black Believer* and McCray's *The Black Presence in the Bible*. Their books go into far more detail and are much richer in content than these humble few pages.

Now, let's continue our journey and see how we might bore through the walls separating us from the inner city and those living there.

CHAPTER 6

Why Not Let Someone Else DO IT?

So the LORD spoke to the fish, and it vomited Jonah onto dry land.

Jonah 2:10

Jonah ran from the command the Lord had given him to go to the great city and preach repentance. He ran to a boat heading in the opposite direction! When confronted with a great storm, he ran from life itself, talking the sailors into throwing him overboard. I believe he planned to die in those waves, forcing God to find someone else to do the "dirty work" of preaching to the Ninevites. But God saved him and held him in the belly of the fish until it "vomited" him out onto the beach.

The New Testament presents those three days in the belly of that great fish as the only sign of Christ's messiahship our generation will be given. Christ's sacrifice for us included three days in the belly of the earth, the grave. Our commitment to Christ and his sacrifice for us is what now takes us to our Nineveh—the inner city—and deposits us on the beach.

Now we're looking at our Nineveh.

And the wall surrounding it is tall, broad, and thick. As we've seen, it's constructed of powerful building blocks—suspicion, fear, and apathy, fed by anger. Our command, like Jonah's, is to enter the city and minister there.

Our Nineveh has no gates. The wall is solid. To enter, we have to cross the invisible line and penetrate Satan's wall. Bore a gate into it. Kick it down. So that we can begin ministering to God's people who live within.

Since apathy dampens the will and produces inaction—and, believe me, we need action—let's take on apathy first.

Let me give you an example of overcoming apathy in order to minister to people's needs. The following example does not come from the inner city, but a more remote area of our country.

SNOWBOUND

In the early morning hours of January 13, 1997, in the four corners area of the United States (where, if the states were empty boxes, you could pick up Arizona, Colorado, New Mexico, and Utah with your thumb and three fingers), the temperature dropped to ten below zero and snow began to fall. The 250,000 inhabitants of the Navajo reservation there are spread out over some 27,000 square miles.

It's a hypnotically beautiful land—red soil stretching forever, painted, flagged rock pushing up, carrying flat mesas on its back—all of it punctuated by towering eruptions of stone, snaking arroyos, steep canyons, and razorback ridges. If you made a wrong turn out there, you wouldn't know it for fifty or sixty miles.

Getting around is a difficult process at best. When many of the Navajo awoke that morning, it became next to impossible. They were snowbound. Almost three feet of snow had fallen, and the drifts, driven by a bitter wind, were six to eight feet high.

Like we have cities and counties, the Navajo have chapters. Those with populations earning their living herding livestock, usually sheep, are little more than a chapter house (or meeting hall) and a few scattered homes and farms. With the snow piled everywhere, the herders found themselves cut off from their sheep and their sheep from food.

Seldom does winter come to this area with the ferocity it did this January. Hardest hit were the children. Families with four or five kids are not unusual. Those old enough to go to school normally have just enough clothing to do that; younger kids have less. Since the homes built out in the rural areas are not well insulated, the lack of warm clothing and blankets quickly became a concern. Most had fuel to heat their homes, but because of the bitter cold they were using it at abnormal rates.

The elderly were also hit hard. I'm getting up there myself, so I can tell you that nothing cuts through aging bones like an icy cold wind. These old people, like the kids, were ill clothed and, being too weak to get to safety, were forced to endure the cold.

The Navajo Emergency Management (NEM) Group quickly called for help. The federal government, the National Guard, and local and national assistance groups responded, as did private citizens. Together with NEM, they went to work to get help to those who needed it most—those farthest from the towns and villages.

Hit particularly hard was the White Clay chapter, a settlement of thirty or so families in a mountainous region just north of the Navajo headquarters at Window Rock, Arizona. The weather precluded the use of helicopters for rescues, so members of NEM got on their snowmobiles and headed up there. But four feet of powdery snow quickly buried the snowmobiles and brought their expedition to a halt. A man suffering from pneumonia was eventually rescued by a Snowcat, a piece of heavy equipment the Tribal Authority uses to service the power lines strung across the reservation.

Another dramatic rescue in White Clay involved two families who tried to escape the snow on the morning of January 14. Two husbands, two wives, a grandmother, and five small children took off in two 4 x 4s (all-terrain vehicles), plowing their way through the deep drifts. But after about five miles, one of the 4 x 4s broke an axle in the mud beneath the snow. Since all of them couldn't fit in one truck, the husbands decided to leave the women and children and try to make it down the mountain for help. They set up a camp using the damaged 4 x 4 and kindled a fire for warmth. It was getting on toward noon when they set out. A mile later, they, too, were buried in the drifts.

As late afternoon approached and the temperatures were beginning to drop below zero, one of NEM's snowmobile teams with attached sleds came upon the men desperately trying to extract their truck. They immediately told NEM about the women and children a mile farther up. By the time the rescue team reached the other party, night was coming on fast and the temperatures were dropping even faster. Although the fire was still going and everyone seemed okay, they weren't dressed for severe cold—not the kind of cold that was surely on its way with the darkness. But the snowmobiles were still blocked by the deep snows and couldn't get the stranded people back to their homes. Even if they could, a trip down the mountain held another danger.

Windchill.

The NEM team debated what to do. If they bundled the people on the sleds, they would be reasonably warm just sitting there. But when the sled started to move, the windchill would cut through their inadequate clothing and could produce severe frostbite. The rescuers quickly decided to send one of their own men down the mountain for help.

Braving the night, the snow, and the subzero temperatures made even more severe by the windchill, one of them made it back to Sawmill, the closest town. He returned on a Snowcat, which looked like a giant yellow snowdragon as it lumbered up the drifts. Piling everyone on board, then gathering up the two husbands, who by now had given up digging out and were huddled in the truck's cab for warmth, they headed down the mountain to safety.

Several stories of such personal heroism emerged, stories of people helping people. I heard about the Navajo's problem not from the news, but from a friend who lives in Southern California, some ten hours from Window Rock. This friend is in sales, with California and Arizona as his territory. The Navajo Nation is one of his customers. He called just after the storms hit and discovered their plight. He decided he could help with warm clothing. Enlisting others in his church, in a single day he collected boxes of winter clothing and coats. After borrowing a van, he and his wife drove the warm clothing out to the reservation—ten hours there and ten hours back. The Navajo, of course, were grateful.

In a five-day emergency period that January, three died due to the snowstorms. State and local governments spent over one million dollars battling the emergency.

Natural disasters can be devastating. But can the damage all be placed at Mother Nature's feet? After all, the people chose to live in these remote areas. They could have lived near towns, or changed professions so they could. The chapters could have kept accurate records of where people lived, so they could have been found more easily. The people could have been better prepared—they could have foreseen that one day they would be faced with such a winter as this.

None of that mattered. People were in trouble. They needed help.

And people overcame their apathy and went to help.

The last thing I want to do is minimize what the Navajo Nation went through, particularly those who lost loved ones. Their loss, no matter how you look at it, was great.

But as disasters in this country go, this was a relatively minor one. We hear all the time about floods washing away entire communities, about hurricanes blowing half the seacoast away, or tornadoes leveling small towns. Billions of dollars in damage; hundreds of lives lost. The toll, in terms of human misery, incalculable. We, as Christians, overcome resistance and come to the aid of people caught in disaster's grip. We send warm clothing, as my friend did, or money, food, medicine—whatever is needed, we try to supply it. We show compassion.

I asked my friend why he decided to help the Navajo. They were so far away, and certainly they would be helped by Christians and non-Christians who were much closer—those in Gallup or Farmington or elsewhere in the four corners area.

His answer was quite telling. "I had to help. There was no choice. The Lord told me that people I cared about were in trouble. I couldn't do everything, but I could do something. So I did what I could."

Just as Jonah was deposited on the beach by the great fish, we're deposited where we can help our neighbors by our commitment to Jesus. My friend acted upon this command.

Well, there's another disaster going on—and for most of us, it's a lot closer than a ten-hour drive. It might actually be in our own backyards. And just as our apathy is overcome to help those in the grip of a natural disaster, it should be overcome by this one caused, in part, by our human natures. This disaster, of course, is in our inner cities.

THE INNER CITY AS A DISASTER AREA

Let's look at this disaster as we would look at any disaster—in terms of its human toll. And we'll look at only one contributor to that disastrous toll, the effects of crime. The following data comes from the FBI.

First, looking at 1995, the last fully reported year, most crime takes place in the large cities—5,761 crimes per 100,000 inhabitants versus 2,083 crimes per 100,000 inhabitants in the rural areas. Not only are there more crimes within the cities, but there is a larger concentration of crime in a smaller area. A hundred thousand people live a lot closer together in L.A. than they do in Flagstaff, for example.

Crime is a way of life in the large city, and with it come the fear and anxiety. In the country, people talk about the fear of tornadoes, hurricanes, or earthquakes. In a large city, you're much more fearful of being mugged or carjacked or killed.

Has anyone in your family ever been arrested? It's all too common in the inner city, and it is traumatic for a family. This person you've loved, lived with, maybe been intimate with, is suddenly dragged off in handcuffs. Maybe you had no idea what he or she was up to. Maybe he's being charged with something truly serious, and you wonder if you really know the person. Could the police have made a mistake? Is he really a thief, or drug dealer, or murderer? There were over fifteen million arrests in the U.S. in 1995. Forty-four percent of those arrested were under the age of twenty-five. Kids. Parents are loving these kids, and an arrest alone, whether the person is guilty or not, is a difficult situation.

How do we calculate the damage? Disasters are always reported in terms of million or billions of dollars in property damage, but property damage merely underlies the severe disruption of people's lives. Homes going up in flames, all their belongings smoldering in the ruins. Or being washed away in a flood.

Their memories, their home businesses, everything that brings stability—it's all gone, or in need of huge sums of money for repair.

In 1995, over fifteen billion dollars in property was reported stolen. These thefts disrupted people's lives, often severely. We can argue that the things stolen were only things, but often these things took hard work to get. Maybe insurance came through and eased the blow, but, in the case of muggings, purse snatchings, and the like, it probably didn't. Maybe treasured memories were associated with the things stolen, or they represented a lifetime's achievement. More important than the actual "stuff" stolen is the sense of violation such crimes bring—the sense of not being safe in your own home, of not being safe anywhere. It takes a strong Christian conviction to get over the desire for revenge.

Even though theft is a terrible thing to endure, it involves only things.

Not so for violent crimes. People are hurt, and people die.

For every 100,000 people in the United States, 685 were victims of a violent crime—murder, rape, robbery, and aggravated assault. Granted there are those who may be evenly matched with their assailants, but not often. Why would someone intent on violence choose a victim who could fight back? No, we're talking about crimes that come at you like a sledgehammer. And, like a sledgehammer, they leave terrible scars, both physical and emotional.

A young lady in her early twenties, who was from a Christian home and was not sexually active, was drugged and raped. She only knew she was raped because she slipped in and out of consciousness during the act. When she went to the police, they told her there was no evidence, since she didn't even have a clear memory of the crime. Now she's pregnant with the rapist's child. Having been talked out of an abortion, she faces living for nine months with "a monster's child in my womb." Through no fault of her own, she has to reassess her college plans and even though she now plans to give the child up for adoption, she must tell her parents she's pregnant. She doesn't know how they'll react, since her father has previously stated he doesn't see how any woman can be raped. There are just too many ways to kick their way out of it, he says. A strange position, but one many men hold.

STATISTICS DON'T TELL THE WHOLE STORY

Life seems to be cheap in the inner city. Thirty percent of all violent crime is perpetrated with a firearm, and far too many bullets are finding their targets—or even, as in the case of drive-by shootings, a random target. Just reciting the death toll does not begin to tell the whole story, but let me first give you some data.

For every hundred thousand people in the U.S., eight are murdered in the average year. When I first read that, it didn't seem like a lot. In 1995 in L.A., according to FBI statistics, 849 people were murdered. I had expected thousands, especially when ten people were murdered in our neighborhood in one month alone. But when you think of how many lives are touched by a murder, the number of victims goes up.

WHY NOT LET SOMEONE ELSE DO IT?

Statistics don't tell the whole story. Only eight people in one hundred thousand may be murdered, but the number of victims is far greater.

Who are the murderers? Strangers killed 55 percent of murder victims. Again the sledgehammer. You go out for a drink and end up in a parking lot, lying in a pool of your own blood. You're stopped at a traffic light and someone kills you for your car. The fear: it might happen to you. Over time, what does that fear do to a person? It has to make us more suspicious of approaching strangers, more aware of where their hands are, the lighting, the others around us, how many locks we have on our doors. It makes us more paranoid. It has to make us more callous as well. For our own emotional protection, we look at life as being a little cheaper. Instead of a murder victim lying there, we see just a curiosity, a morbid interruption.

But there are times when it's impossible to protect ourselves from what we see. Two young boys from St. Stephen's were out walking after school and approached an intersection. A man stood there waiting for the light to change. When they got within a few feet of the man, he suddenly pulled out a knife and slit his own throat. What a thing for young eyes to see. No amount of time or counseling will erase that image.

Husbands or boyfriends killed 26 percent of murder victims; wives or girlfriends, 3 percent. Suddenly homes are shattered. Mom is cooking dinner and Dad comes in and blows her away. Mom goes out on a date and leaves the kids with a baby-sitter and never comes home. One minute children are members of a family, the next minute, wards of the state. Mothers and fathers have grown kids with homes, families, jobs, futures, and suddenly it all vanishes in the smoke of a gun. What does this say to women, or men, who are in abusive relationships? Should you stay just to remain alive? If you leave, should you start wearing full body armor? A husband who had just lost a divorce judgment shot and killed his wife in front of their children in an L.A. courthouse.

Murder. The toll is devastating.

And bigger than any disaster—21,597 people were murdered in 1995 in the U.S.

Granted, not all of them were in the inner city. But, for the sake of argument, let's say half of them were (a number I think low): that's more than forty-five TWA Flight 800s falling out of the sky in a single year. By anyone's count, that number alone labels the inner city a disaster area. And it leaves us with something quite irrefutable: just like our dear Navajo friends, the inner city needs our help.

What kind of help do our cities need? Sending in the National Guard might help stem the tide of social ills, but when the Guard leaves, those ills might just return. No. This disaster area needs the gospel of Jesus Christ.

And if you don't help bring it, who will? There's no time for apathy now.

Do you remember the uprisings in our cities thirty years ago? They began in the spring and summer of 1968, with the tragic deaths of Dr. Martin Luther King and Senator Robert Kennedy, and lasted all the way to 1972. They were called "the long, hot summers."

Leading up to those terrible events, our church, in league with many others, had been ministering to the inner city. We had established day-care centers, K–12 schools, a homeless program, outreach programs to our youth and to the elderly. We had times specifically set aside for prayer, something I'll deal with in another chapter. When those tragedies burst upon us, because of our presence in the community, our Long Hot Summers remained reasonably calm.

Even against the furious tides of social unrest, the love of Jesus Christ, brought by his people, can prevail.

GOD'S PROTECTION

Danger lurks in the inner city. We've just seen the statistics. Within the walls, the fear can decay a life as surely as liquor or drugs. And for those outside, it can lock you out.

As you read this, your fears are probably heightened. I've painted a picture that shows you what people within the inner city are going through, and I may be scaring you. Although there is reason for you to be cautious, there are many ways to minimize your risk in ministering to the inner city.

First, go in the daylight. Also, go with someone who is part of an existing ministry and knows his or her way around. You'll quickly find that you're as safe there as anywhere. After all, if you are called to ministry in the inner city, you are there on God's mission, and God's angels are protecting you.

One night our entire family—my wife, five sons, and I—was leaving the church grounds. An assailant, hiding in a sprawling bougainvillea, threw a brick-size rock and shattered our windshield. Sharp shards of glass sprayed over the entire family, but none of us were injured.

Another incident, one that evoked a great deal of fear, occurred one Sunday morning during the worship service when a note was passed forward to me in the pulpit. The note said that three men had given a criminal five thousand dollars to kill my sons. We quickly gave this information to the police, who instituted the necessary protection.

On the Monday following, the man came to make good on his threat. On television we're told that we can see angels, that they present themselves as such and help us as if they were social workers. Well, maybe that's true. It certainly seemed true for me that morning. My wife and I were meeting with two plainclothesmen in my office, discussing this very matter, when the would-be assailant arrived. He was quickly arrested. He had told someone just that morning that he was going to use the large-caliber handgun police found on him to "get some money from Pastor McKinney." His plan: to rob the church and, before leaving, do away with me and my family. Investigation showed that he was perfectly capable of succeeding on his threat. He had spent seventeen years in New York's Attica prison for murder and was still a very dangerous man.

Jonah was in no greater danger than when he was thrown bodily into the boiling sea, yet God had work for him and protected him.

God has protected me, and my work for him, on more than one occasion. As a bishop, I oversee sixty churches. One of them wanted to buy a new facility, so the pastor engaged a consultant to help raise money for the acquisition. The consultant, in turn, engaged an appraiser to appraise a new property. But the consultant was a crook; he pocketed the ten thousand dollars meant for the appraiser and skipped. When he wasn't paid, the appraiser went nuts.

Because I was the bishop, he came after me. He began by writing threatening letters. When I didn't hand over another ten thousand, he started making phone calls. The last one went like this: "You've got until tomorrow to pay or you're dead—you and your entire family—your wife, your kids, their wives. See, I know about their wives. You got till tomorrow."

I called the police and the FBI and decided the best thing was to cloister my entire family somewhere else.

Meanwhile, the threatening calls kept coming. Sometimes fifteen or sixteen a day. This went on for a whole week, when finally the FBI got hold of the man. They must have been effective, because the threats ended and we were able to come back home. It's frightening enough when your own life is on the line, but it's terrifying when your family is in danger.

Of course, it's also terrifying when the whole neighborhood is in danger. There are times when the police will come by the church and caution us to stay indoors because bullets are flying around outdoors. Whenever that happens, I can't help but think of those who don't hear from the police and might unwittingly step in front of one of those bullets.

With access to food and crawl space during storms and darkness, the inner city is also home to another threat: the mentally ill, many of whom are no longer institutionalized and therefore homeless. Because they

99

are so unpredictable, it's quite disconcerting to become the object of their attention. I've been stalked at least three times. Since they were on foot, they didn't follow me home at night, but they were there when I came to the church in the morning. Standing there, staring. Eyes vacant and yet the windows to something deep and dark going on inside.

Once one of them who had been stalking me came into church on a Sunday morning. While I was preaching, he slithered along the side wall until he was halfway to the pulpit. Then he began walking with purpose—what purpose, heaven only knows. But no one stopped him, and he got within a few feet of me before I stopped preaching, pointed a finger right at his face, and commanded, "Stop and sit down in the name of Jesus Christ." He did. I felt my heart start again, and I finished the sermon while some of the ushers helped the gentleman out of the church.

I'm not sure how this next story will sound, but I'll tell it just as it happened in the hope that you will understand. To begin with, I am not a large man; I'm about five–five, 160 pounds. We were in the middle of a praise service, a wonderful service filled with joyous singing and praise for our Lord, when this large woman—250 to 300 pounds—stomped in. As she marched from the back of the church all the way to the front, she was swearing. A mad-hornet kind of swearing—demon possessed—foul. I commanded her to stop. She didn't. I commanded her again. She got worse. Finally, shaking a finger at her, I told her: "I will not allow our worship service to the Lord to be interrupted like this. And this is my Father's house; I will not allow language like that."

She only got louder.

Suddenly I felt the Spirit of the Lord come upon me, and my blood boiled. Then, like Jesus going after the money changers, I came out of that pulpit and knocked that woman down. Some people said I flipped her. Now remember, she was a big woman. I stood there crouched like a sumo wrestler, waiting for her to get up and start the next round, when the woman rolled to her knees before the pulpit and started repenting, loud sobs of repentance and horror at what she had done. Whatever had possessed her had gone.

I knew the words of Psalm 23 in a vivid way: "Yea, though I walk through the valley of the shadow of death, / I will fear no evil; / For You are with me" (v. 4).

A dear friend of mine is a missionary to Colombia, the home of the drug cartels. If there is a violent city anywhere on earth, it is Colombia. Even judges hand down their decisions anonymously, protected by bulletproof cocoons. I once asked this missionary if she was ever afraid. "No, not really," she said. "I won't die until God wants me to die. And I can't imagine I'd be walking down the city street one day and God would snarl, 'Get her.'"

Fear is real. But so is God's protection.

Does that mean you're absolutely safe? No. But as God's children, we know that our lives are in God's hands. And just as Jesus gave his life on the cross for us, there may come a time when we will be called to do the same for him. Our assurance, though, is that our sacrifice will be for his glory, and he will make "all things work together for good."

Therefore, fear should never stand in the way of our ministry. If it does, we deny God's power over darkness and his promise that to be absent from the body is to be present with him.

So. Overcome the fear. Take it a little at a time—baby steps—maybe start with a visit to a church in the inner city. Attend a service, or meet with a pastor, take a walk with him. Meet members of the congregation, go with them as they minister. Learn, then take part.

What if you suspect their motives?

Suspicion is the easiest obstacle to deal with. Naturally you suspect their motives, suspect they don't like you or don't want you around. So what? Isn't that true of any unsaved person? Wasn't that true of you when you were unsaved? Your motives were suspect, you were always out for number one, you didn't particularly want your Christian friends (if you had any) spreading the gospel around your feet.

When they come to a saving knowledge of Jesus Christ, you'll suspect them no more.

Apathy, fear, and suspicion should no longer be keeping you from ministry in the inner city. But there's another reason to overcome those three building blocks of Satan's wall.

SO THAT MEN WOULD SEEK HIM

The Los Angeles of 1997 is much different than the Los Angeles of 1897. The pressures were different a hundred years ago. Worries were different then. The things that might kill you were different. Social mores were different. Those things that might cause someone to look deeply within himself and determine that he needs a Savior were different. The Lord, knowing us more intimately than we know ourselves, knowing what it would take for us to seek him, chooses the time and place we will be born as part of his creative act. Someone he placed in L.A. in 1897 might be a very different person from someone he places there today.

The same is true of Los Angeles, California, today versus Delano, California. Delano is a farming region with far different pressures and concerns from those affecting someone living in downtown L.A. today. But God knows that, and it's part of his divine plan.

"From one man he made every nation of men, that they should inhabit the whole earth; and he determined the times set for them and the exact places where they should live. God did this so that men would seek him and perhaps reach out for him and find him, though he is not far from each one of us" (Acts 17:26–27 NIV).

This verse tells us that God's people are being placed in the inner city so that their lives there might cause them to seek the Lord.

And that is further proof that God has not abandoned the inner city. Quite the contrary, the inner city is there as an environment where certain of God's people are placed so that God's beacon might shine in their eyes.

Remember Miguel, the young man who sold one of the drugs in a speedball that killed a teenage girl? Had Miguel been raised in Delano, had he been given farming work—kept busy from dawn till dusk—he might never have experienced the searing guilt that turned his eyes toward his Savior. What about the guy who laid the sawed-off shotgun on the altar of our church one Sunday morning? Had he grown up on the beaches of Maui, surfing and catering to tourists, he may never have had to look inside himself and been revulsed at what he saw.

Romans 8:28 tells us that "all things work together for good to those who love God, to those who are the called according to His purpose." I believe that "all things" includes *where* someone is.

Since God has placed people in the inner city so that they might seek him, because of their particular physical, psychological, and emotional makeup, it gives new life to another verse in Acts. In a vision, the Lord spoke to Paul to keep him from leaving Corinth: "Do not be afraid, but speak, and do not keep silent; for I am with you, and no one will attack you to hurt you; for I have many people in this city" (Acts 18:9–10).

What was Paul asked to do in Corinth? Preach the gospel. For it is by hearing the gospel that the ears are unstopped, the eyes are opened, and the word is planted in the hearts of his people.

Such was true for the people in Corinth, the people in Nineveh, and it will be true for those you decide to help in the inner city.

So we must expend the energy to break through the wall and preach. But exactly what are we to preach? Let's look at that next.

CHAPTER 7

How to Share the Gospel in
THE INNER CITY

The word of the LORD came to Jonah the second time, saying,
"Arise, go to Nineveh, that great city, and preach to it the mes-
sage that I tell you."

Jonah 3:1–2

Since I've been in the gospel business for fifty years, pastoring for the last thirty-five years, I've met a lot of diverse and interesting people. Within these pages you've met a sampling of them. Many came to a saving knowledge of Jesus Christ while I knew them. With some I had the divincly given privilege of leading them to Jesus. I learned something from those opportunities.

The gospel is a single message: Jesus, the sinless Son of God, came to a spiritually and physically fallen earth to die in the place of his people so that they might be reconciled to God the Father.

Jonah was commanded to preach the word God gave him. Like Jonah, we're commanded to preach the gospel of Jesus Christ.

One thing my thirty-five years in ministry has taught me is that although it is a single message, various elements of the gospel appeal to the hearts of different people, usually according to their needs at the time. Just as God gave Jonah the message to preach— "Repent or in forty days judgment comes!"—we, too, are told what elements of the gospel to stress. God gives us that knowledge as we learn about the person to whom we are witnessing; because of our love we ask questions so that we might understand what that person's needs are.

Let's look at some of those people and the elements of the gospel that might be stressed.

LOVE

Because of the rampant use of heroin and the high incidence of homosexual behavior in the inner city, many of those living there have contracted HIV and, subsequently, AIDS. Areas known for their homosexual populations are being devastated.

And those with AIDS could be considered modern-day lepers. As a society our reaction to them has been similar to the reaction to lepers in Jesus' day. We shun them and give them little sympathy. Jesus did not react to lepers that way. Quite the contrary, he met them where they were and healed many of them.

I was determined that St. Stephen's would follow Jesus' example.

Many in the Christian community had decided that AIDS-sufferers would not be welcome in their churches.

I can only chalk that up to fear that some of their members might contract the disease and fear that by inviting in those suffering from AIDS they might have to deal with the whole issue of homosexuality. I was determined not to fall prey to that fear, so I announced to the congregation that St. Stephen's would welcome those being ravaged by that disease. As it turned out, some of my members were not immune to those fears. Several were sure that I had overstepped my bounds. I was equally sure that I had not.

Jesus prevailed.

We decided to reach out to those troubled individuals and their families. First, we established an open door: we would welcome and love anyone with AIDS, or anyone living a life that would place them at risk.

Churches and homosexuals have never been close. The homosexual sees condemnation from the church, and the church sees—well, I'm not sure what the church sees, but whatever it is, it's something they want no part of. I've always regretted that. If there is a group anywhere that can benefit from seeing the love of God, it is homosexuals.

Homosexuality is a sin. It's identified as such in the Old Testament; in those days it was punishable by death. But it seems that there's something particularly noteworthy about it. God points to this sin when he shows the total depravity of Sodom and Gomorrah. He also points to this sin (homosexuality and other sexual perversion) in Judges 19, to show how far Israel had fallen away from the Lord.

The New Testament talks about God giving a nation over to such perversions (Rom.1). Homosexual sin seems to be a bellwether, a touchstone that gauges the spiritual health of a nation. Homosexuality probably exists whether the nation is spiritually healthy or not, but the gauge is the nation's reaction to it. In a spiritually unhealthy nation, homosexuality is condoned and even encouraged. God's word on the matter has been removed from the equation in that nation.

Our country may have already arrived there.

As a sin, homosexuality separates a person from God. But, as with any sin, heartfelt repentance washes the sinner clean and reconciles him or her to God.

Our open-door policy at St. Stephen's allowed us to witness firsthand God's saving grace being extended to homosexuals.

Stan had watched his male "roommate" die from AIDS; then Stan was diagnosed with it himself. Rejected by his mother, father, and two older brothers, he abandoned himself to a small apartment not far from the church. He could have taken advantage of many support groups, but he decided against them. Having felt alone most of his life, he wanted to be totally alone now. Stan was in his mid-twenties. His younger sister, Marcie, was fifteen. Marcie, a Christian, had been a member of a youth group at another church for about a year. When she heard that our church was welcoming people like her brother, she suggested he begin attending.

One day when Stan was feeling particularly vulnerable, he consented to come to one of our services. It was a Wednesday night, and he sat with Marcie in the very back. Over the next few months Stan came now and again. The first few times he came with Marcie, then he showed up on his own. Not regularly, but often enough to be exposed to the gospel of Jesus Christ.

Stan was failing fast. AIDS sufferers don't die of AIDS; they die of some other disease that a healthy immune system can usually reject. Stan was losing weight and was frequently in the hospital for one thing or another. Marcie was constantly worried about him. As God's grace began to work in Stan's heart, he began to open up to Marcie's love. What makes loners loners—homosexual or not—is an inability or an unwillingness to let the love of others into their lives, perhaps to protect themselves from being hurt. Now, as Stan saw his days dwindling, his loneliness became overwhelming—and he could stand it no longer.

As I understand from his mother, Stan's rebellion started at an early age; even before he could walk he was known for testing his parents. One of the symbols of that rebellion was a ragged gray-and-pink elephant an aunt gave him when he was three or four. It was a ragged old thing, gray and floppy with a trunk that was attached to the battered body by only a few sturdy strands. When he started kindergarten, he asked his mother if he could take the elephant to school. She said no, and Stan exploded. Whipping the elephant around his head by its trunk, he slammed it to the floor. When told to pick it up, he refused and screamed that he would never touch it again. His mother expected him to forget his oath—after all, he was only five. But he didn't. His mother, being just as stubborn, also refused to pick it up; she kicked it into the corner of his room.

109

There it lay. Now and again his mother would vacuum under it, but she refused to put it away. And, as Stan grew, he also refused to touch it.

It became almost a joke among the kids. But it was no joke to Stan and his parents. Touching that elephant would be an act of surrender for Stan and triumph for his parents.

As he lay dying in the hospital, he asked Marcie to get the elephant.

When Stan's mother saw Marcie leaving with it, she immediately knew something was up. Although Stan's father still refused to get involved, Stan's mother followed Marcie to the hospital. She had hopes that she and her son would finally apologize to each other and be reconciled. Stan did apologize. But he also told his mother, with Marcie present, that with the help of the hospital chaplain he had repented and invited Jesus Christ to be his personal Lord and Savior. Since his mother was not a Christian, this was his first and, as it turned out, his only verbal witness. But his nonverbal witness became thundering.

Since he was dying and could hardly speak, I felt it a privilege that he honored me with a few minutes of his time. Just before I left, I asked him what it was about Jesus that finally brought him to understand God's grace.

"He loved me," he said simply. "No matter what I was. I couldn't push him away. He showed me his love through Marcie."

She was with us when he said that, and at the mention of her name she clasped his thin, weak hand. Less than a day later, while she still gripped that hand, he died—confident that Marcie's hand was Jesus' hand.

I made sure he had a glorious Christian burial, and he went to his Lord washed in the blood of his Savior, one arm holding his ragged gray-and-pink elephant.

Stan responded to the gospel message when he saw the love of Christ demonstrated. Another element of the gospel that the inner city needs to hear is forgiveness.

FORGIVENESS

In the last chapter we saw the statistics on violent crime in the inner city; we saw that many people are touched by it. Add to that number those touched by the common lapses in human civility—like injustice, disproportionate rage, misunderstandings, all those things that wrong us, that deserve retribution or at least an apology—and we end up with an incalculable number of people who are angry with one another and who desperately need to forgive.

A lack of forgiveness can turn people hard. It can put them on a destructive track to revenge. It gnaws at their insides, robbing them of a lot, maybe all, of life's inherent joys. Although many cherish their anger and the power they feel it gives them, others realize its destructive nature and would dearly love to get rid of it. But it's hard without the Lord. There's something very seductive in holding on to the notion that one day, somehow, justice will be meted out; we want to be there to relish that moment of justice.

So we preach forgiveness, often in soft, loving tones. But, as with love, preaching it without living it produces a hollow sermon indeed. This is particularly true for the church leadership. Although the Lord has been gracious to me and I've not had to forgive what others have been called upon to forgive, I have been able to set a small example.

June graduated from San Diego State University and, in spite of the fact that she had a husband and two young children, felt she was called to the ministry. I found her a bright, articulate woman and thought she would succeed in whatever she tried. We put her on a program of preparation, something all of our ministry candidates must submit to, but she didn't want to complete the program. She wanted to plunge right in to full-time ministry. I counseled against it. She rejected my counsel and, leaving her husband to baby-sit full-time, she headed off to do domestic missionary work. She quickly ran out of money and began passing bad checks to support herself. After I heard about it, I called many of my colleagues to let them know she was working without my blessing.

When she found that none of our churches wanted her help, she sued me for "interfering with her livelihood." In court we argued that, as a bishop, I have certain responsibilities, among them attesting to the suitability of those working in the vineyard. We won the case.

Soon thereafter, her family began to disintegrate, and I lost track of June for a couple of years. Then I received a call from her. She was desperate and living on the streets. I have to admit, forgiving someone who had spurned my counsel and then sued me for doing the job God had given me was not the easiest thing I'd ever done, but God had disciplined her far more thoroughly than I ever could. I recommended that the church pay for a few nights' lodging while she got herself together emotionally, then we all welcomed her back into our fellowship.

Such a story of forgiveness, however, pales in comparison with the following.

Willy James Jones had just graduated with honors from a local high school and been accepted at a prestigious Ivy League college. While at a local graduation party, Willy James was gunned down in a drive-by shooting. My heart still aches just to think of that terrible loss. His grandmother and aunts attended St. Stephen's, and I was called to join them at the hospital when they went to identify the body. He was such a strong, handsome lad with such a bright future— the pride of us all.

A year and a half went by, and no one was arrested for the crime.

The mother of one of the lads in the car from which the shots were fired also attends St. Stephen's. When he was no longer able to live with the guilt, he told his mother of his involvement. As she states, "Because of the training I received at church, I gave my son two alternatives. Either he would tell the authorities what he'd told me, or I would."

He did, and his confession led to the arrest of the triggerman. It was a high-profile case here in San Diego, and during the trial there was a huge outpouring of love and support for Willy James's family. But it was the family themselves who showed a true Christian spirit. As the trial grew to a close, they publicly expressed their forgiveness for Willy James's killer.

But forgiveness is not a one-time thing. The anger can return.

Dr. John Isaac Davis, associate minister at St. Stephen's, lost his adult son to a spray of gang bullets in 1987. One evening this son told his ten-year-old daughter that he had an errand to run and would be right back to play with her. He never came back. The errand was to deliver a meal to a sick lady up the street. As he approached the lady's house, he was caught in a hail of bullets from a gun battle between two rival gangs. Shot eight times, he died there on the pavement.

Dr. Davis has his Doctor of Divinity degree in theology, so he knew he had no choice but to forgive his son's killer. But knowing and doing were entirely different things. Making it more difficult was the fact that his son's daughter, his granddaughter, took her father's death very hard. She is now an adult, but Dr. Davis still cannot tell her he "will be right back." The memory of that night is still too brutally vivid.

Dr. Davis knew forgiveness had to start with prayer. So, gathering his wife and granddaughter around him, they prayed long and hard for forgiveness. And it was just as hard in coming; the rage was so strong. But by the time of the murderer's trial, he had a sense of it within him. It was a good thing, too, for the trial lasted six weeks, and every day he had to face the killer. And the killer had no intention of making it easy on him. He was constantly making arrogant, contemptuous faces at Dr. Davis, and he even threatened him once. Dr. Davis is quick to admit he actually welcomed the thought of the guy coming after him—just to get his hands on him. . . .

More prayer. More communion with his Lord over Scripture.

The jury found the killer guilty, and he went to prison.

Dr. Davis had to get on with his life. And after more prayer and more immersion in Scripture, the sense of anger and hate dissolved. Forgiveness had come. Healing began.

Dr. Davis's healing was helped immeasurably by encouragement from an unexpected source. His son had been a building contractor and had hired many young men from the inner city. For many of them, it was their first meaningful job. After his son's death, many of these young men came to Dr. Davis and thanked him for what his son had done for them. Men he didn't even know would take him gently by the hand and tell him how much his son had meant to them. Two told him that it was his son's urgings that had kept them off drugs.

Nothing will replace his son—nothing—but the knowledge that his son was a good Christian man softens the blow and provides this father with pride no mere gangster's bullet can take away.

But sometimes the rage returns, Dr. Davis says. Unexpectedly it grabs his heart and chokes it. He relives the moment he first heard the horrible news; he finds himself breathing fast, feels a curse catch in his throat. Suppressing it all, he begins praying again. Such a moment came when the prosecutor told him the killer had been released after serving only six years.

More prayers. More Scripture. One in particular. Romans 8:28: "And we know that all things work together for good to those who love God, to those who are the called according to His purpose."

Dr. Davis says it helps to talk about it. There's a sense of release in telling the story, connecting with someone who for just an instant feels what he felt. Forgiveness is important for our witness, our hearts, our physical and emotional well-being, and we should practice and preach it fervently. But it doesn't take away the pain—nothing really does—we just get to a place where we don't think about it so much.

Some of those who have been wronged see the anger and hate inside that is eating them alive. But in their own strength they're unwilling or unable to do anything about it. When they see God's people forgiving the unforgivable and going on to live triumphant, joyous lives in Christ, some want to experience that for themselves. Forgiveness is not only something we preach to those who need it, but something we live so that they might see its value firsthand.

But there's something else about showing the world how we are able to forgive. Great forgiveness, as in the testimonies we've just read, is so foreign to the natural human condition that there is something miraculous in it. Revenge and hatred are such a part of our bones that when they are removed, we are literally showing the Lord at work in us in a mighty and personal way, particularly if the Lord has placed us in a public forum.

In addition to love and forgiveness, another powerful way to present the gospel is to show how every person has a purpose in Christ.

JESUS GIVES PURPOSE

When I met Candace she was in the holding cell, waiting to be charged with attempted murder. Her pimp had brought the charge. He said she had attacked him with a toaster, swinging it by the end of the cord, hitting him several times in the head and knocking him unconscious. When he came to, he put the word out on the streets and eventually intercepted Candace at the bus station. He was about to drag her off when a security guard interfered. Thinking quickly, the pimp started screaming about men's rights and how this woman had beaten and knocked him out and he wanted her arrested.

Although I don't personally do it much anymore, I went down to visit the prisoners that evening, and that's where I found Candace.

I couldn't tell how old she was; I guessed mid-twenties. She looked very hard—ink-black hair, gray eyes, chiseled expression, wire-drawn lips. I could see how she would be quite effective when swinging a toaster. But something else was quite out of place with her; she was frightened. Although I didn't know it then, she expected to be killed any minute—either by a cop on the take or by one of the five others in the holding cell. If she was behind bars, she figured her pimp could probably have her killed. She actually called me over so that if someone was planning to take her life they would see me as a witness and back off. I was her shield. I didn't know that either. I just thought the Lord was at work again—which, of course, he was.

I wore a black suit and clerical collar, so it's obvious who I was. Prisoners don't like surprises.

"Hey, Padre—I always liked it when John Wayne said that—hey, Padre —"

She spoke quickly, her tone tight like a guitar string. She did manage to get a John Wayne flavor to the last "hey, Padre."

"Hello." Often I'm a little ill at ease when ministering to women, and talking to a prostitute who was about to be charged with a violent crime did nothing to put me at ease.

"Talk to me," she said, her expression no less hard but more animated. "Wanna save me?"

"You want to be saved?"

"I want to be out of here."

"How'd you get here?"

It was a strange question for me. Normally I would have said something like "I can imagine" or "At least you're not on the street." But I didn't. And my question stopped her. Her expression faded from forced animation to a softer, darker reflection.

"I don't know how I got here—"

I sensed a guard nearby. I knew him, and he offered an interrogation room to us. "Talking will be a little easier," I said.

The interrogation room was small, gray, and furnished with a table and four hard, wooden chairs. She sat across from me and now she seemed to soften.

"I got here by knocking out my pimp. Smart, huh? Well, I am smart. You know how many units I need to graduate college?" She waited a beat. "Two—it's probably more now. They add them as time goes on, but once I had only two."

"You never went back?" I was still nervous. My wife would have been calling her "Honey" and leading her to Jesus by now. I was just sitting there, asking dumb questions.

"I talked them into letting me graduate with my class. I was supposed to take the classes that summer. But instead I decided I wanted to—well, you know." She stopped there.

"Have you ever done anything like that before?"

"Like what? Quit when I'm close? No—yes. Jobs. You don't really care about this. You just want to put another notch on your Bible. I don't know how many of you people I've talked to in the past few years. Coming out to the street corner and handing things out."

"What jobs?" I asked.

"In college. I majored in social sciences. How many people do you know who actually work in their major? I do." She laughed, a tight sort of laugh. "I went to get a job at a lawyer's office. I told them how good I'd be. Got the job—paid good. But then never showed up. I turned my first trick [she used another term] the night before I was supposed to start. I started hookin' in college. It was fun in college."

"Where did you grow up?"

"Talking about—work—make you nervous?"

"I regret you've taken those roads. It's hurt you."

"It's my choice, isn't it? I've made all the choices. My dad used to sit around all day pitying me. 'Poor Candy—poor, poor Candy,' he'd say every time I hurt myself. But I made the choices. It was me that went out with the guy that got in the accident and killed a kid—I just thought I'd throw that one out there. I like to see your eyes pop."

"Did they pop?"

"Like a stomped-on toad frog." She said that like Tennessee Ernie Ford. She looked too young to mimic him. "You ever see a dead kid?"

I had, but there was no reason to tell her about it. I shook my head.

"The guy I was with was so excited about scoring with me that he drove down this hill like a maniac, met some kid driving up the other side, and forced him off the road. The kid hit a tree. Blood everywhere. 'Poor Candy,' Dad says, 'having to see something like that.' Poor me? I was alive. He should have grounded me forever. But they were my choices—right? Mine."

She told me about a few more of her choices. Hitchhiking and escaping being raped only because the guy hit his head on the rearview mirror and for an instant was distracted. Waterskiing with a guy known for his drinking and nearly being beheaded by an overhanging branch. She showed me the scar above her hairline.

"You're trying very hard to destroy yourself," I finally said. "Any 'customers' ever get rough?"

"Some."

"And beating up your pimp . . . isn't that a capital crime in your circles?"

"Why do you think I called you over? Nobody would dare hit me with you around. I'm safe with you."

I smiled. I wanted to let her know just how safe she truly was with me. "I think you called me over to hear about Jesus."

"Sure. Right. You bet!"

Although she faced death outside, after I mentioned Jesus one more time she banged hard on the interrogation room door and told the guard to take her back to the cell. I guess she's no different than most people out there; they'd rather face death than face Jesus. Of course, one day they're going to end up facing both.

In the inner city many are slowly, systematically destroying themselves. Instead of putting guns to their heads, they're making choices that put them at increasingly greater risk, until they finally make that final choice.

What does Jesus offer them?

Purpose.

People destroying themselves like this see no value to their own lives. And, in a twisted way of proving it to those who might care, they treat themselves as if they were of no value. They throw their lives away.

But they are valuable to Jesus. He calls his people according to his purpose, then prepares good works in advance for them to do. He has a mission for us. A divine mission. And when we become his, we begin to live our lives as if our lives have value. Because they do. What Christian, when he knows he's in God's army, fighting God's battles, would intentionally throw his life away? I wish I'd had the chance to tell Candace that. It might have made a difference.

Not only does God offer purpose to those in the inner city, but strength. "God is our refuge and strength, / A very present help in trouble" (Ps. 46:1). That's a message people living in the city desperately need to hear.

OUR STRENGTH IN TIMES OF TROUBLE

Romero has a wife and two small kids. He's in his midthirties, having waited to get married until he felt reasonably secure financially. By inner-city standards, he is. He works two jobs, both in security. He heads up security at a manufacturing company not far from the housing project where he and his family live. He also works as chief of security at the housing project.

The place is built in a squared horseshoe around a courtyard, forty units on three levels. At one time this complex sparkled with flowers and shrubs. Now, where anything grows at all, it's nothing but weeds. The remains of a children's play area is off to one side, a rusted swing and a broken merry-go-round that doesn't whirl anymore.

Romero believes that things can get better. When he first saw the place, he pictured the flowers sparkling again—saw a new swing set—saw the neighbors and their kids enjoying the courtyard together.

He also saw the drug dealers and gang members evicted from the place and other families like his own moving in. The first week he was there, he took the security job; actually he demanded it. Romero intended to make a difference. Although his wife was worried for his safety, she only voiced it once. She'd been married to him for five years, and she knew his determination.

Romero's first move was to make friends with the police at the local precinct. They, too, wanted to clean out the bad guys and they welcomed Romero's involvement. They promised to respond to every call he made as quickly as they could, which was a major commitment on their part. In a large city the police are seriously overworked. Unless someone's life is threatened, or there is the overwhelming probability of big property loss, the police are nowhere to be found. But, now, on Romero's call, they would come.

Next he talked to the housing authority and found out what conditions he would need in order to evict: police-generated proof of serious lawbreaking going on and the occupants would be out.

Realizing that he was often a bull in a china shop, Romero said nothing more to the tenants. He decided to lie in wait, and he didn't have to wait long. A third-floor tenant beat up his wife, a loud, violent altercation that nearly had him throwing her over the railing. Only Romero's cry from the center of the courtyard stopped the guy. The police came, found about a pound of coke in the guy's place, arrested them both for possession with intent to sell, and then kept them away long enough for Romero to effect the eviction. Within a week a new family had moved in. A single mother with three kids.

Romero knew he was on the way.

He evicted two others, both for drug violations.

His wife began planting flowers. With his own money he bought a new swing set. Several tenants helped him assemble it, and that night they had a little party in the courtyard.

But they weren't out of the woods yet. The party turned into a major drunk as other tenants tumbled from the apartments and crashers from outside the complex arrived. Romero and the "good" tenants were severely outnumbered and just retired, leaving the party to the bad guys. When a fight broke out, Romero called the police. For the first time they were slow in arriving, but they did arrive finally and the party broke up—for the time being.

About three in the morning the partying started again, accompanied this time by gunplay. Romero

woke to the sound of gunfire—quick, explosive, terrifying—six or eight shots. Then six or eight more. He
leaped out of bed and stood in his doorway, watching
shots being fired and returned from a second-story
apartment to one on the third floor. Maybe two apartments up there. It was hard to tell from where he stood.
His wife had already called 911, and the police were
on the way.

A cry. Was someone hit?

Sirens. Red and blue bubbling lights.

The gunfire stopped.

Police everywhere. Romero pointed to the second-
floor apartment, and seconds later the police converged on it. They also headed up to the third floor
and converged on an apartment that had attracted a
number of bullets. A call came down that someone
was injured. The police called an ambulance, which
showed up minutes later. Romero didn't see who was
injured, but he later heard it was a guy, probably a
gang member. A bullet had grazed his head and taken
off part of his ear.

The police arrested a guy in the second-floor apartment and took him away.

Before the police left, they told Romero to be careful. They were sure they had not gotten everyone
involved. For Romero that was a very disturbing truth.

Not only were people who had been involved in
the shooting still in the apartment complex, but everyone had seen Romero working with the police to get
gang members arrested.

His wife also knew this, and she expressed her concern for him and her children in no uncertain terms.
He tried to reassure her, but he was too worried to be

convincing. Romero lost all credibility with her when a bullet splintered their front door the next morning and lodged in the living room wall. Their toddler had passed through the living room on the way to the kitchen only minutes before.

He reported the shooting, but with no witnesses—no one had come forward—there was nothing the police could do. Again they told him to watch his back.

The next couple of days were terrifying for Romero and his family. There were more gunshots—one through the window, a couple through the door. A small plastic bag of blood was splattered against the wall near his door. As if to show him there was nowhere in the apartment he or his family could hide, a brick was tossed through their back bathroom window, spraying broken glass all over the tub and tile floor.

The kids were constantly in tears. His wife was trying to figure out places they could go, but they were even afraid to use the car for fear that it might be booby-trapped.

They called the police after each incident, and with each call the police seemed more distant. There were too many things in the city they could do something about, and those things, obviously, had to take priority. When Romero told them he was afraid to use the car for fear of a bomb—

"You say there's a bomb in your car?"

"I think there could be."

"Oh—could be. Well, take a look and make sure. If there is, give us a call."

When Romero went around to the other tenants, the ones who had supported his efforts in the beginning, he found them aloof and unwilling to get involved.

They didn't want bullets flying through their doors. He had a hard time blaming them.

Romero and his wife had been raised Catholic. Neither were very close to the church, but suddenly they found themselves praying. According to Romero, their prayers seemed forced and empty. Like a waste of time, and yet he couldn't bring himself to believe that they were.

The third night they got a phone call.

A Hispanic accent: "Better get your kids out of there, man. Or they're going to be toast."

Romero had been a marine, and something inside him refused to let him run. But that threat seemed too real to ignore.

They called the local Catholic church. Maybe if the priests were praying for them—maybe they had more clout with God—if there was a God. Nobody answered the phone there, and they suddenly felt very alone.

They put blankets over all the windows. Now no one could monitor their movements, and any thrown objects, like a Molotov cocktail, would be stopped from reaching the interior of the apartment. About ten at night, the kids asleep, the place dark except for the glow of the television, Romero and his wife curled up on the couch and tried to feel brave. Only a few minutes later, they heard a commotion outside. Someone laughing and singing, then laughing again.

Over his wife's objections, Romero opened the front door to investigate. One of the tenants, a friend, was on his way home. He was falling-down drunk. Beside him, trying to help, was a young man Romero knew as one of the administrators of a rescue mission a couple of blocks away.

"I'm sorry, Romero," the young man said. "I found him about a block from here. I'm just trying to get him home."

"I'll help. And when you get done with him, I think I need to talk to you."

A few minutes later, the young man of God spoke with Romero and his wife. Eventually he prayed with them and shared the gospel with them, particularly God's promises that he's our God in times of trouble and hardship. He read Psalm 91 to Romero, who said, "Trouble is already at my door, Pastor."

Romero was not saved that night, nor was his wife, but they did have a taste of the Lord's protection. About four that morning, long after the young pastor left and Romero and his wife crawled wearily to bed, they were awakened again, this time by a sharp, official rap on their door. When Romero opened it, a policeman stood there, one he had never seen before. They needed the key to a couple of apartments. It seemed there had been a shooting involving the tenants of those apartments, reputed gang members. Two were dead and three others were being held. They needed to collect evidence.

With those tenants gone, the threats to Romero ceased. His wife began planting flowers again.

Romero is open to talking about the gospel now, and we are all praying for him and his family.

THE GOSPEL MEETS NEEDS

Love, forgiveness, purpose, protection, strength. These are elements of the gospel that people in the inner city are hungry to hear. Like people everywhere, they need to discover that Christ meets them at the point of their need.

For the young mother trying desperately to work, feed her kids, and provide a roof over their heads, the Lord is her provision.

For the parents of a murder victim, Christ is their comfort.

For that drug user who seems to wander from one high to another, Jesus is a lamp unto his or her feet that guides, one day at a time, along the straight and narrow path.

Just as Jonah knew that going to the Ninevites and calling for their repentance was an act of love, I believe we show our love for the people to whom we are witnessing by learning enough about them to put the gospel in life-relevant terms.

So as you think about ministering in the inner city, you might think about which elements of the gospel can be emphasized. We've discussed only a few of them here. I'm sure you can come up with many of your own. Start with how the Lord presented the gospel to you.

Now that we've examined which aspects of the gospel you might be able to present, let's explore *you* a little bit. What talents do you have that the Lord can use? Do you have a gift to share?

CHAPTER 8

Do You Have a Gift TO SHARE?

So Jonah arose and went to Nineveh, according to the word of the LORD. Now Nineveh was an exceedingly great city, a three-day journey in extent. And Jonah began to enter the city on the first day's walk.

Jonah 3:3–4

Now, if I've made my case that the inner city needs your help, how should you respond?

You could just send money. All ministries need money. And all of us should be financially supporting ministries we believe in. Without money, ministries end up ministering to themselves. Of course, if you want to send St. Stephen's money—go right ahead. We'll put it to good use.

But, as wonderful as it would be to receive those donations, I am convinced that true progress will only be made in the inner city when people in sufficient numbers inside the wall come to a saving knowledge of Jesus Christ, and people from outside the wall come personally in sufficient numbers to make a difference. Only then will the wall be obliterated and the people truly set free in Jesus.

The question, of course, is, How do you get involved?

Scripture is clear: God equips his saints.

Jonah was a prophet, one who proclaimed the word of God to a lost and dying city. That was his job. The Lord gave it to him. Prophesying was his gift. He was probably given other gifts as well. Courage to actually go to an enemy city, to face being swallowed by a "great fish," to endure the kind of storm his ship endured. He was probably given a firm speaking voice, one with volume and authority. Strength for the journey. A quick mind to handle the unexpected. And whatever other gifts were needed to equip him fully as God's servant.

We're all equipped in some way. What about your gifts?

But before we get into that, what is a gift, anyway?

Just about anything can be a gift. A wonderful voice, the ability to organize, a head for financial matters, a "green thumb." A spirit of calm in the heart of turmoil. Courage. An eye for detail. A sense for the positive. Anything that furthers God's kingdom and gives comfort and encouragement to God's people is a gift.

So the territory is pretty broad. What's more, a gift can be quite obscure. A young lady had a dark mole— a beauty mark—located in such a way on her face that it gave her a wonderfully unique look. It caused an older man to comment on it one day and, in turn, gave her the opportunity to witness to the man about God's grace to her. Although she never saw the man again, she was able to share Jesus with him. At that moment the mole, or beauty mark, was one of her gifts.

Usually gifts are a little more recognizable—the ability to listen and understand, to relate to kids or the elderly, to articulate an idea clearly, to write or speak, to sing (so people want to listen). And just as yellow and blue combine to make green, a combination of gifts makes another gift, a unique ability. For example, Peter relates well to kids, and he and his wife open their home to foster children. He is also a fine baseball player. So Peter not only helps kids, but he helps them as only love and encouragement on the field of competition can.

DISCOVERING YOUR GIFTS

In a way, Jonah had it easy where his gifts were concerned. God just spoke to him. Told him what to say, what to do, and where to go. That's not to say Jonah was some kind of a robot, but, at least with one of his gifts—prophesying—it was God who identified it and made sure it was used, even when Jonah rebelled.

It's a little different with us. Not many of us have heard an audible voice telling us that we have the skills to paint great pictures or gently juggle five infants in the church nursery. No. We actually have to think about our gifts and, perhaps, go through a process to identify them.

So, why don't we begin that process right now?

First, make a list of things you are good at. Be complete. I knew a right-handed young lady who could stand firmly on her left foot. Although there were times I saw her stumble over the carpet in the church hallway, she could stand on that one foot with such perfect balance that I doubt if a tank could dislodge her. If you have a skill like that, put it down. Also put down the more obvious ones: "I enjoy math; I crochet; I love to cook; I dance like Michael Jackson; when I saw my first comet through a telescope I was thrilled." You know the things that belong there. Take your time and leave nothing out.

Now, from that list extract another list. What have others said you were good at? If you think you're a good cook, have others agreed with you? If you put down that you're good at math, have teachers said you were as good as you thought? If you've put down one of those "standing on my left foot" things, have there been times when others have marveled at that ability in you?

In other words, which of your talents have been confirmed?

A gentleman was once asked to leave the choir. He couldn't understand it. He thought he sang wonderfully. And because of that belief, he sang with all the gusto breath afforded, even when the music was marked *pianissimo*. But he did not sing wonderfully. In fact, he sang horribly off-key—so far off-key, he was singing a different song. The choir leader dubbed him "the struggling locomotive." As time progressed, he became disruptive. Choir members began to complain, and though he was asked to tone it down, he didn't. He was sure others were just jealous.

Now this man undoubtedly had other gifts, but singing was not one of them. So keep in mind that God's gifts will be recognized not only by the bearer but by the recipient as well.

Modesty will also play a part in keeping our lights under bushels. Be honest. If you're good at something, admit it. So what if you're not the best? Not everyone is a Michael Jordan or Shaq, but he or she makes tremendous contributions just the same.

Now that you've identified those things you enjoy doing, and those that people have confirmed you do well, there's something else. To minister effectively you not only need a gift, you need love.

A HOOK OF LOVE

One of the great thrills of my life was leading Darren to the Lord. Only in his mid-thirties, he had already been quite successful in business. Even before he came to know the Lord, Darren was known as a fair, honest, and hardworking man—someone you'd want your children to emulate. When the Lord brought Darren in, he attacked the Word voraciously, just as he approached everything in life. He read at least four chapters a day in Scripture, studied several commentaries at a time, and was forever asking me and others on the staff questions. And they were thoughtful questions, those born of a growing understanding of the deeper things of God.

"I want to teach," he told me one day, about six months after he'd been baptized.

"I'm not so sure that's a good idea," I said. I had seen others newly on fire for the Lord want to help others whom they now saw as lagging behind them. A noble idea, if all there was to teaching was teaching facts.

"I'm ready," he insisted. "I've done a study on the Holy Spirit and I want to teach it."

"The Lord warns us not to go too fast."

133

"I've been studying six months. I was only in business a few weeks before I was teaching the new people what I'd just learned. I'm ready."

"Darren, I counsel against it."

"Well, I'll just have to show you I'm ready."

My minister of education was eager to use him the moment he opened his mouth, because teachers are not easy to find. It's hard, often thankless work, and the risks are great; Satan has a real stake in your failure.

So Darren started teaching.

Two months later he sat before me, his head drooping. "You were right. I wasn't ready. I'm still not ready. The questions come a mile a minute and I'm just not prepared to answer them."

"Is there anything else?" I asked.

He looked at me for a moment, wondering if it was a trick question. "Well, they are a frustrating group. They fight about the dumbest things, and when I step into the battle at least one side disagrees with me, sometimes both. It's maddening. Sometimes I want to throw things."

"I had a feeling that was the case."

His head cocked in curiosity. "You've taught that class before?"

"You don't love them."

"Love them?" He burbled and hissed like a teakettle. "How can you say that? You know how much time I spend preparing for that class? Researching—putting together the lesson plan? Hours into the night. Plus, I can't go away for the weekend anymore. I used to go fishing sometimes, but I need to be here every Sunday. Love them?"

Teaching wasn't his gift. If it had been, he would have loved his students.

After all, when all is said and done, the Lord's chief complaint about Jonah was that he didn't love the Ninevites. He had no desire to see them receive the Lord's grace, and he fought the Lord every way he could.

In the case of a teacher, or with any other gift that includes working with those you want to save, loving your students drives you to understand how to instruct them. Instead of an enemy you have to force-feed, they become Christ's children. And he has entrusted their spiritual nurture to you. The love this perspective produces causes you to look beyond the silly questions, beyond the confrontations, the frustration, and the anger. It drives you to come up with what it takes to get the job done. Oh, there are times when even the truly gifted give way to frustration or even anger. But, on the whole, their hearts burn for those they're ministering to. They have the true burden.

So when we ask ourselves what gifts we possess, we also must ask ourselves, Do I truly love those to whom I've been called to minister?

A middle-aged man who had been an alcoholic much of his adult life came to know the Lord. When he did, the Lord severed his emotional tie to booze. With the emotional tie gone, the physical dependence was cut more easily. After months of sobriety, he felt he had a lot to offer those currently struggling.

His witness was simple. *I did it; you can too.*

Since the inner city boasts plenty of substance abusers, he quickly found a place to minister. Not long after he started, a young woman from his class came to see me. She was distraught. She had been sober for about a month and then tumbled off the wagon. Courageously, she had come to the class for honest help and encouragement. Instead, she had been belittled. The knife the young lady would use to cut that thick, tough tie to booze had been severely dulled.

I went to the next class; the young lady was right. At times a mentor has to be tough, particularly when straightening people up and getting them to do the difficult things in life. A marine drill instructor comes to mind. But even a DI doesn't treat his guys with contempt.

Why did the woman fall off the wagon? What can she do to avoid slipping again? If it happens again, what should she do? Loving her would have caused him to find out, maybe even to call her later to make sure she was okay. He would have held her hand through a tough time. He would have been a surrogate Jesus.

As with anything, there are degrees. If you're teaching a ceramics class, or bringing together local artists for an art fair, or assisting some math students, or bringing your bunny rabbit to a kindergarten class for show-and-tell, the illustration of the marine DI may be overkill. But you get the idea.

Every true gift of God hangs on a hook of love.

When love abounds, even less than perfect gifts can rise to incredible heights of service. So it was with Carol. She made porcelain dolls and did beautifully delicate work. To be brutal, the dolls she made were not of a professional quality. But they were very nice, usually good enough for a second or third place at the local fairs. As an outreach, Carol decided to hold classes. While she taught the ladies, she talked about God as a creative God and how he is revealed in his creation. Her favorite expression was, "If it's this difficult to make a person out of clay and paint, what must it be like to make one of flesh and blood and brain?"

The people joined in, all of them talking and laughing as she worked caringly with each one. When a lady came who had made porcelain dolls before and was actually a little better at it than Carol, she welcomed the woman, at times even elevating the visitor's instruction above her own. In doing so, Carol won her over. By the time the class ended, everyone who came saw Jesus' love at work in Carol, and, therefore, at work in themselves. Many of the ladies continued to come to church, and, over the years, several were saved.

Now let's get back to your list. It should just about be complete. But before we leave the subject of gifts, there's one more thing I'd like to say. God often uses our gifts, particularly the passion associated with them, in our own sanctification process. In a real sense he gives them to us not only to use for others, but to use on ourselves, to bring us closer to him.

USING OUR GIFTS ON OURSELVES

Elizabeth painted pictures, mostly in oils. Delicate works—lacy curtains swept by spring breezes, butterflies dancing on sparkling rays of sunlight. She had a remarkable talent. But no one knew. She painted in an extra bedroom, and when people came to visit she closed the door and blamed the smell of paint and thinner on a decorating project that never seemed to end. In moments of weakness she thought about entering her paintings in the local fair but always decided against it. Friends might see them and realize she had the talent.

It wasn't arrogance that kept Elizabeth from sharing her gift.

It was fear. Fear of criticism. Fear that under criticism a fragile ego might crack, perhaps disintegrate. So much of herself was wrapped up in her talent—her gift—that it was as if she, herself, were on the canvas. Every brush stroke, every color, every subtlety, every grand design came from so deep within her, from so many secret and vulnerable places, that when her work was complete, a very personal part of her was on view. If anyone criticized the painting, they were criticizing that very vulnerable part of her.

This is especially true of young artists. You've probably seen it in yourself at times, or your kids. We write a poem, or draw a picture, or write a paragraph that somehow deeply reveals who and what we are, and we hide it. Or, if we show it at all, it's to those we know will not hurt us.

Do you have gifts like that? Things you're good at, but because they are so much a part of what you are, you don't dare reveal them for fear of setting yourself up for a fall?

Write them down.

Remember, you're a child of the King. You, like the rest of us, are imperfect; but you are also his, and your imperfections are forgiven. Your life's work is to live for him and to work for his kingdom goals. If you're reluctant to use a gift where it might make an impact, it's time to speak to your pastor or a Christian counselor and deal with those things within you that are keeping you and your gift from being useful.

SOME GIFTS ARE KIND OF SILLY

Cath writes, well, things. Like—

> *I love eggs*
> *with legs*
> *and hats that a fat cat lacks.*

and—

> *Millie Pumpernickel*
> *takes a nickel,*
> *buys a pickle that he squishes with his 'cycle;*
> *sells the brine for a dime.*

They're silly. She admits it. But they just seem to spill out of her—some would use the word *seep*. She'll be sitting at dinner and start writing them on a napkin, three and four at a time. Words tumble onto the paper, bouncing, colliding, spinning to rest like hubcaps—oops, I'm beginning to sound like her.

Is this a gift? Why not? There's not enough silliness or fun in the inner city. Do you do something like this? Draw cartoons or funny pictures? Sculpt silly animals, people, things? Believe me, you can be used.

OTHER WAYS JESUS USES
OUR GIFTS

Meg was in her mid-thirties. Married. No children. A committed Christian, she had been coming to St.

Stephen's for nearly two years. Meg seemed to live a fulfilled and productive life. She worked in classified advertising for a local newspaper, something she enjoyed, and was married to a great guy. In the two years I'd known them, I had never heard a harsh word pass between them.

But something was wrong. Meg seldom laughed. And deep in her eyes, on those few occasions when I had time to study them, I detected a resident sadness— a darkness of soul—like shadows covering a grave of lost hopes.

One afternoon when she brought by some posters to promote a church function, I suddenly saw that sadness lift—only for a moment—when she glanced over to our little children's play yard. Five kindergartners were playing on the swings and in the sandbox, and they were having a boisterous time.

Meg smiled. Broadly. And I swear I saw a bit of moisture at the corner of her eye.

Frankly, I'd always thought she didn't like children. She had none of her own, and she had refused to help out in the nursery every time she was asked.

But there was no mistaking what I had just seen.

I couldn't let the moment pass. After all, people hide so many things from their pastors—things pastors are put on earth to help them with.

I gently took her by the upper arm and said, "Come with me."

Realizing she'd been caught, and probably a little glad for it, she followed me to my office.

We spent about an hour together. The conversation began with Meg again trying to hide the deep feelings she had buried for years. "No, I really don't

want kids. I don't like kids that much. I was just notic-
ing how cute they were. But puppies are cute, and I
still don't want the responsibility for house-training
one."

But I had seen the look she'd given those kids. It
came from secret places.

I asked Meg about herself, about what it was like
growing up. I asked about her parents, her brothers
and sisters, what she liked to do. I asked about her tes-
timony. And I noted something. Even though we were
talking about very nonthreatening things, her voice
was becoming tighter and tighter, her posture more
withdrawn: arms folded defensively across her chest,
shoulders pulled in on one another, protecting her
heart. It was as if something inside her was fighting to
be seen, while another part of her was fighting even
harder to keep it under wraps.

"Have you ever been pregnant?" I asked.

"Yes," came the reply. It hung there for a moment
on gossamer threads.

"Miscarriage?" I pressed.

Her head shook.

"Did the child die?" My voice was charged with
empathy.

"You could say that," she said, and in her evasion
she related volumes.

"Tell me about it."

"It's not important anymore. I don't want to bring
it up."

"It *is* important. You love children, and you've not
forgiven yourself for, well —" We pastors love our pop-
psych, and we're often right. Love makes us right.

We've been given eyes for things. But in this case I wasn't entirely right.

"I do love children."

"—and you haven't forgiven yourself for aborting one. How old were you when it happened?"

"Old enough to know better—twenty-two. I was in college. I was a Christian. I know all about forgiveness."

"But not for yourself. Why didn't you just have another child?"

"I can't have any more children."

"Why not?"

"The abortion did some permanent damage."

"I'm sorry to hear that." More sincere empathy. My hands clasped in front of me. "What about adoption?" I was pressing pretty hard. To Meg's credit, she did not storm out of the room. But she did remain tight.

"Jesus doesn't want me to have children. I obviously wouldn't make a good mother—or maybe there's some other reason. He just doesn't want me to have children."

"Has he closed the door on adoption?" I asked.

"We never tried."

"Then why don't you?"

"Because he's obviously closed the door on me."

Now I knew. "Perhaps you haven't forgiven yourself, but you've also not forgiven Jesus—have you?"

She looked at me. Her arms rose and fell as her chest began to heave. Turmoil grew inside. Her eyes remained fixed. Finally she said, "I wanted kids more than anything in the world. More than anything. And I loved God more than anything. I remained a virgin.

I wouldn't let any man even touch me. Then I slipped, one time—and wham—I'm pregnant.

"I didn't know what to do. I was only a semester away from graduating. My folks would have taken away all my support. I decided abortion was my only way out. Then there were complications, and I learned I could never have kids. I had served God faithfully for nearly seven years. I make two mistakes, and he cuts me off from the one thing I always wanted. It's just not fair. He's supposed to forgive us.

"I go by those kids down there two or three times a week, and my heart just breaks. How could God do this to me? I was a Christian. His child. I wouldn't be that cruel to a child of mine. Why did he punish me so hard?"

There were more tears and a little more talk. I had one of our professional Christian counselors call on Meg, and she ended up going through about a year of counseling before she finally realized again how loving our Lord truly is.

The Lord gave Meg a gift—a towering, passionate love of children—and then placed himself directly between her and that gift. The longing for what the gift provided her was the carrot that drew her through that meadow of disenchantment, took her on that journey that ended where I hope we all end up: in total love and surrender to our Lord.

That's a place I'm not sure Jonah ever got to.

Do you have a passion like this? One you deny because Jesus, for whatever reason, has kept you from fully pursuing it? Maybe there's some spiritual work you need to do, or perhaps he's just been waiting for this very moment. If you can identify that passion, put it down on the list.

Meg now helps in the church nursery on a regular basis, and she and her husband have decided to become foster parents; they are currently taking the state-sponsored classes. Where before Meg refused to acknowledge her gift, now she is using it in and for the 'hood.

SO, WHAT'S THE NEXT STEP?

The subject of gifts is vast and we've only scratched the surface here. I encourage you to read more on the subject or talk to your pastor. Another source of good information is those in your church or circle of friends who have excelled at things that take hard work and commitment—artists, writers, performers, executives of large companies, or entrepreneurs who have built something from nothing. Talk to them about their gifts and what they've learned about using them. Then ask them how they might use those gifts in the inner city. Challenge them.

Of course, now it's time to challenge yourself.

It's time to go to the Lord and ask him how he wants you to use your gifts. Let's talk about prayer—what yours should be, and what God's response might be.

CHAPTER 9

Praying
for the
INNER CITY

Then Jonah prayed to the LORD his God from the fish's belly.
Jonah 2:1

Early in our ministry the deacons of the church came to me. "Pastor, we think you're working too hard, and we'd like to take over the financial aspects of running the church—paying the bills, things like that."

Well, of course, I was delighted. Paying the bills did take time I could easily put to better use. So I handed the checkbook over and began filling that time with other things.

About three months later, the deacons handed me a notice from our bank. The bank was foreclosing. The mortgage had not been paid since I had handed the checkbook over.

"Fellas," I began, "I took you seriously. You said you were going to pay the bills. What happened?"

They fidgeted a bit, their eyes glancing around the room. "Well, we were embarrassed. There wasn't enough money to pay all the bills."

"Then why didn't you tell me? I could have tried to do something."

There was no answer. Now I wasn't sure what I was going to do. We needed five thousand dollars, and we needed it by Monday. This was Friday. We put out an urgent plea to the congregation and raised about five hundred dollars. Only $4,500 to go! We got together as many members as we could and prayed. On Sunday, when I gave my sermon, I preached as if our prayers had already been answered—as if the money was already in the bank.

Sunday evaporated without another dollar coming in. Half of Monday did too. Then I got a call. It was from a gentleman I had never met, a wealthy man who lived in La Jolla, an upscale area of San Diego. "Bishop McKinney," he began, his tone hesitant as if he wasn't really sure what he was going to say. "I've been hearing about the good things you're doing there for the people, particularly the youth, and I was wondering if there was anything you might need."

"Well," I said, as I felt my heart and eyes begin to fill, "I need five thousand dollars."

"That's all?" he said.

The bank got his check the next day.

You can understand, then, why I pray a lot. I pray when I want something, when I'm thanking the Lord for something else, when I'm in despair, when I'm praising the Lord, when I want the Lord's blessing before I start a meeting or project, for traveling mercies (something I often need), and when I feel alone.

I also think a lot about prayer and its function. Why, like the example above, is the answer sometimes immediate and truly miraculous? And why, like in some of the examples to come, does it sometimes seem to bring no results at all?

In 1962 mine was still a tent-making ministry. I was working full-time as a probation officer and also full time as a minister. Our congregation consisted of only eleven adults. The largest tithe was fifteen dollars a week. But to grow, we needed a facility and a plot of ground to put it on.

The congregation prayed, and I started looking.

First we found the plot of ground. It was ideally located, just the right size, and cost far more than the twenty thousand dollars we had.

We estimated we would need another twenty to thirty thousand dollars for a building, bringing the total to around fifty thousand dollars. We prayed some more as I kept looking.

A newspaper ad pointed me toward the coast just north of San Diego. A church there wanted to sell a building and have it moved, clearing a plot of land so they could build an even larger facility in its place. The first time I set eyes on it, I knew the church would be perfect for us. It was beautifully appointed and large enough to seat a hundred people. It was ideal. But they wanted five thousand dollars for it. I told the pastor who we were and what such a facility would mean to our ministry. "Really—well, then. For you the building is free. You'll just have to pay to have it moved."

A couple of quick calls and we found that we could move the building to the lot (which we still didn't own) for five thousand dollars. So for twenty-five thousand dollars—half of what we first estimated—we could have a church that would seat one hundred people in San Diego's inner city.

The eleven adult members met; we prayed some more.

That facility also meant something else to me, something that caused me to pray even harder. It meant I would finally be able to quit my day job—being a probation officer—and concentrate on my first love: service to my Lord. Over the preceding years there were times I'd pray for hours, asking the Lord to put enough money into the collection plate so that I could quit my day job and be a full-time minister. I longed for that day. If you, too, have a ministry that only supplies a part of your needs, you know what I'm talking about. It's like living two lives. Every morning you wake up with two "to do" lists. And you work wearily into the night, often giving waning energy to your first love, always wishing you could do more.

I began to tell my associates at work what we were trying to do. The word spread. More people began to ask questions and get involved. People I didn't even know called, and within six weeks we raised the twenty-five thousand dollars.

Prayer takes many forms in Scripture. We see the grave, yet fleeting, requests of Nehemiah. We see long, confrontational prayers like that of Habakkuk, or great prayers of praise and surrender like Mary's Magnificat.

Then there was Jonah's prayer: "Jonah prayed to the LORD his God from the fish's belly" (Jonah 2:1).

No prayer occurs in a stranger place than Jonah's: from the belly of the great fish. I think God is showing us in this prayer that he is with us anywhere, no matter where we are going or what we are doing. Even if we're in rebellion like Jonah, who, at the time, was literally being dragged back on course.

My hope is that you're about to embark on what will be an important and rewarding journey: your attempt to make a difference in the inner city. Many souls are at stake, as well as your well-being and the well-being of many committed ministries. Prayer is certainly in order.

But what should you be praying for, and what answer should you expect?

THE COMPLEXITY OF GOD'S REPLY

In the first chapter, we saw how the Lord answered our prayers after our church was torched, how he took us in directions and blessed us in ways we hadn't dreamed of. In a very real sense, our ministry became his. What we wanted, the directions we wanted to go, were suddenly secondary to where God wanted it to go. None of us prayed for a tent, yet he supplied it. None of us prayed for national recognition, but he supplied it, as he did the seeds for many new ministries. Of course, we're quick to point out it was his ministry all along; perhaps he just wanted to remind us.

Even before he spoke to us from the flames and ashes in 1984, he had spoken to us from a large hole in the ground, back in 1967.

I was in full-time ministry by then, and the facility we had moved onto our property was now too small. We had filled the hundred seats and needed hundreds more. But we were still a poor congregation, and any facility expansion would take far more money than we had or would ever hope to have—except through another one of God's miracles.

And, since God had miraculously brought us our current facility and had, with an equally astounding miracle, filled the place in five short years, surely he would provide even more.

It was time for another step of faith, and I was eager to make it. For the sooner I made it, the sooner I would see the Lord work. And I lived to see the Lord work, especially on my behalf.

As the summer warmth of 1967 broke in steamy waves across south San Diego, we broke ground. After all, it took no money to begin digging. And as we dug, we prayed. We prayed for money. For donations of building materials. For workers to help build. We prayed with raised hands and voices, and as we prayed, we dug. By summer's end we had a 60-by-100-foot basement dug, and we were waiting on the Lord to miraculously turn that hole into our new facility.

Days came and days went and the Lord did nothing. It was as if he'd ceased to exist—gone silent—stopped caring.

The hole remained. And as the days clicked away, leaving the warmth of summer in favor of the apple-crisp air of autumn, it seemed to speak louder than the Lord. The hole seemed to be jeering at us.

"Okay, Bishop, where is he?" it was saying. "Thought he was going to be doing something to me. Making me into something grand, something eye-popping. Making me into something that would really get those new people coming in. I'm still sitting here waiting." It was like an audible voice, and I heard it every morning as I parked my car beside that hole and headed for my office. Every time I took a break and looked out my office window. Every night before heading home. I was sure it was screaming at me.

One day it seemed to be screaming even louder. A couple of guys from the neighborhood stood near the edge of the hole, laughing. They dubbed it McKinney's Folly. I was now a laughingstock.

Although it didn't occur to me until a few hours later, as I sat staring blankly at some silly sitcom on television, it was the Lord's doing. I had taken a step of faith. I had assumed the Lord wanted our work in the inner city to grow—something I considered a truly safe assumption—and the Lord had made me a laughingstock.

And, in a real sense, he'd done it at his own expense. For even though they were laughing at me, they were really laughing at him.

There's a wonderful moment in the Old Testament when the prophet Elijah defies Ahab and Jezebel and challenges the priests of Baal to a little contest to show them the power of our Lord. The contest was pretty straightforward. The four hundred fifty priests of Baal against Elijah and his God. Each side would place a sacrificial bull on an altar. Each would then pray to his god to devour the sacrifice by fire. The god who did would be the most powerful. Well, the four hundred fifty priests of Baal prayed and prayed and prayed, whipping themselves up into a frenzy. Nothing happened.

Elijah then had buckets and buckets of water poured on the altar just to make the Lord's work a little harder. He lifted up his arms and prayed to the Lord. With a blazing tongue of fire, the Lord reached down and devoured the sacrifice, proving to the witnesses—to

Ahab, Jezebel, and the four hundred fifty priests, whom Elijah had slaughtered a few minutes later, by the way— who he really was.

Well, as the days passed and McKinney's Folly remained, I felt like Elijah might have if he had lifted his arms to heaven, prayed, and then nothing had happened. "Okay, Lord," he might have said, "any time you're ready." I could imagine Elijah's self-conscious grin to the crowd after about fifteen minutes.

California has a rainy season in the winter. Where the rest of the country is white, California is soggy. In November the rains came, and the 60-by-100 hole became a swimming pool. There were jokes about diving boards and holding the next Olympic swimming trials there. One guy suggested we build a duck blind and get some decoys. "Charge fifty cents a shot. You'd have this church built in a couple of months, and you could feed the ducks to them homeless people." He laughed, slapped his leg, then walked away laughing even harder.

I could feel myself getting bitter, and many of my prayers included a plea for understanding. I felt like Noah in reverse. He was building a boat on dry land, and I was trying to build a dry church in a swimming pool.

Then, as 1968 dawned, after six months of looking at that hole, after a congregation-full of prayers asking the Lord to please, please bless our church-building efforts in the coming year, something even more terrible happened.

The chiding turned to indifference.

The jokes ended.

When people passed the hole, they didn't even look at it!

Before, they were at least aware of our ministry. It meant enough for them to wonder what was going on. Granted, their curiosity came out in jokes and ridicule, but often such comments were just their way of safely inquiring about the Lord, a way for them to ask what the Lord was doing without appearing to be interested. (If they came right out and asked, it would imply they believed, and many would rather die than admit that.)

Now they didn't even care. They had written us off.

The rains continued, as California rains do. Nothing too harsh, but wet enough to keep the water level in McKinney's Folly constant and the trash that had been thrown in there afloat. Enough to give the occasional duck a safe haven. Well, maybe not so safe.

One morning an old golden retriever who pranced around the 'hood, probably thinking of better days, dug under the protective fence we'd erected around our "pool" and dived in after the ducks. As the mad romping and splashing after those feathered creatures raised his spirits, it inflated mine a little too. At least something was benefiting from our groundbreaking nearly a year before.

It was now April 1968. No one had stepped forward with any money to move our project along; no one was even talking about fund-raising anymore. All our efforts had failed. There was even talk of filling in the hole. Obviously, the Lord was saying no to our expansion plans.

On April 4, he said no to someone else's ministry too.

Dr. Martin Luther King Jr. was murdered.

At that moment, it was as if the heart of our ministry stopped. There were tears, dreams shattered, hopes pulverized. Many cities erupted in violence as blacks everywhere felt that bullet tear through their own flesh. Our city remained reasonably calm. But it wasn't an easy calm. It was an angry, frightened calm, a calm resting on the edge of a precipice: the slightest shove could send it careening over the edge.

I preached calm. I preached our hope in Christ. Others preached it with me. But I, too, was angry. I found myself taking Dr. King's murder personally. I had so many hopes for my church. I saw the new facility as a foundation from which we could launch even greater ministries in the city: more child care to reach the adults, a K–12 school to reach the kids, an energized homeless ministry, more people in the pews. And the Lord had reduced those hopes to a hole in the ground and now a dead leader.

As the months wore on, my depression grew. Why had God answered all those prayers and then said no to this one, this most important one?

Then a glimmer of hope appeared. Sen. Robert F. Kennedy's staff accepted our invitation for the senator to visit our church the evening of June 4, the night before the California primary. *At last,* I thought, *the Lord is at work.* I could see the attention our ministry would get with this visit. I could see the donations flowing in. I could see our ministry back on track.

At the last minute, Senator Kennedy had to cancel his visit. My brother did get to meet him that night in San Diego at a rally, but that was very far away from where I thought the senator was needed. Again my hopes were postponed. I spent much of that night in prayer.

Of course, by the same hour the next night, Senator Kennedy was dead, the victim of an assassin's bullet.

The good senator had a great following within the black community, and his assassination—coming directly on the heels of Dr. King's murder—was that shove I feared. I no longer had the luxury of feeling sorry for myself. My city was about to erupt. But before I could preach a single sermon, two things happened in quick succession: a wealthy man stepped forward, one who had seen our hole in the ground, and handed us a check for ten thousand dollars. "For materials," he said. "I want to do something positive for you folks."

Then another stepped forward. "Pastor, there's so much anger here. If we don't direct it into doing something positive, it's going to explode right in our faces. I'd like to make the building of your church that positive thing. I know I can rally the people here: we can get the businesses, students, politicians, and people from all over the community involved. I know it'll work."

Truly, before I knew it, the man had made good on his promise.

He did get the businesses involved. He did rally the neighborhood. Students, politicians, housewives, professionals and laymen. And within a few days the fence was down, the pool was drained, and building was going on. We even had a white executive from IBM bring his teenage son to work. "I want him to work side by side with black people—all kinds of people. It's important that he do that."

By the time the rains came again, we were in our new facility. Granted, it was little more than a shell of a facility, but the sanctuary seated six hundred people, and there was a roof over our heads and room to grow the ministries we envisioned. As it turned out, it would take about six years of constant work to complete it.

And so the story of the big hole, McKinney's Folly, ended.

If I were a man of perfect faith—or even near-perfect faith—I would never have doubted my Lord. I would never have become frustrated, would never have felt belittled or ridiculed. I would have said, "Listen, ye of little faith, you just watch that hole and you will see the Lord work miracles here."

But I'm not a man of even near-perfect faith. And I praise God every day that he's gracious enough to put up with me and use me anyway.

The Lord is at work in our lives all the time, but sometimes we can't see what he's doing until we look back and see his footprints—the longer the look back, the bigger the picture, the grander the view of his purposes.

In the case of our swimming pool, he was not only working in my life, but my congregation's, and my community's lives. And, when you consider the cost in lives and property of the other cities hit by the civil unrest of that summer, he was also working in the life of the nation.

So, God's reply to my prayer was also a reply to countless other prayers by countless other people, some close by, some a continent away. As you can imagine, replies like that can be complex, with many shadings and subtleties. As you pray for the inner city, be aware that not only will your prayers be answered, but the prayers of the ministries, church leaders, other workers, and even community and national leaders as well. A mosaic of prayers will be considered and finally answered.

So the reply may be exactly as you want but implemented in ways you could never even imagine, or nowhere near what you want but implemented in such a way that God's wisdom is clearly shown, or with many shades in between.

In the case of our hole in the ground, God's reply gave us a new facility, but it also met the needs of a volatile community. Nothing quenches rage more than doing something positive with it. Before long it is smothered in love, friendship, and a sense of purpose.

The last thing I want to do is give you the impression that there were no other churches involved. St. Stephen's was the focal point and perhaps the catalyst, but we were a group of churches working and praying for our community as a whole. Because of those efforts, our neighborhoods had something positive to expend their energies on, and there were no riots here after those tragedies. God's people—God's love—prevailed. And it prevailed with the community's eyes on his church.

And so he will prevail in the ministry you are praying for. Isn't it exciting to watch God work?

I believe that's one of the main purposes of prayer. Like a streetlight, it focuses our attention on areas of our lives where he plans to work. Therefore he works in the light, where we can see him. Otherwise we might miss it—things would happen and we'd probably not even notice. Or we might be tempted to attribute his work to something else. He wants us to see him working in our lives, not only because he wants to assure us he's near, but, I believe, for another reason as well.

GOD WANTS US TO KNOW HIM

My boys don't like me to tell stories about how they act at home. I invariably ascribe motives and thoughts to them that they claim to be untrue. So let me tell you about a friend of mine and his children, two boys and a girl.

He says it's fun to watch them around Christmastime. They will go to any length not to make him angry at them. Starting about Halloween they begin lobbying for gifts. The boys are into electronic games and sports equipment, while the young lady wants the latest clothes or CDs. His youngest boy, who is also the youngest child, decided he would dearly love a Nintendo and several games. Since the gift was expensive, he started the campaign soon after he went back to school in September. He got very specific about what he wanted.

As Christmas approached, he began his bribery efforts in earnest. One morning the parents found warmed muffins by their bed when they woke. The two boys shared a room; every morning after the kids were off to school, the mother found the youngest's side of the room freshly cleaned. Arguments about television shows never included the youngest anymore—he was in the kitchen right after dinner, helping to clean up the dishes.

About a week before Christmas, the presents under the tree still did not appear to include a Nintendo, so the youngster started a desperation ploy. The moment he entered the house after school, he told his mom he would prepare dinner—hamburgers and milk shakes, something at which he was reasonably proficient.

That was too much for his sister. The mom overheard her saying, "That stuff doesn't work with them. You'll have to show them you won't spend your life in front of the television playing games when there are other things you should be doing. Frankly, they don't care how much fun you think you'll have. They want to make sure you don't grow up to be an idiot—even if that's already a lost cause."

In this case, his sister spoke the truth. The reply to a child's request for an expensive gift like a Nintendo tells the child something about the parent. If the parent buys the gift for the child because the child has buttered the parent up, then the parent is gullible and easily swayed by the child's desires rather than his needs. But if the parent doesn't buy the gift—and instead buys the child something educational—the child knows the parents care about his intellectual future.

The same is true for God. How God answers a prayer tells us about him. Through prayer we learn that God is a planning God, a wise God, a knowing God, a God who perfectly orchestrates events, a God who loves us and uses us. Prayer is a way for God to reveal himself in special ways to us, his people, firsthand. If someone tells you God is a forgiving God, you might agree. But when you sin grievously and see personal evidence of God's forgiveness, when he washes that sin away and you see only good come out of it, then you know in your heart he is a forgiving God. And that's where your witness comes from, your heart.

So, as you pray, prepare yourself to see God work and to know him better—both magnificently exciting prospects.

But what about prayers that seem to go unanswered, prayers like Calli's?

UNANSWERED PRAYER

Calli had a tragic past. When she was nineteen and unmarried, she had an abortion; at twenty-two, still unmarried, she gave another baby up for adoption. Having recently come to a saving knowledge of the Lord, she and her husband did a lot of praying. They finally decided to help young ladies struggling with the same issues Calli had struggled with. They contacted a crisis pregnancy ministry nearby and offered a room to any young lady who chose to carry her baby to full term and needed a place to stay. Following the advice they received, they struggled over the rules they would have the ladies follow, sometimes discussing it late into the night. They furnished and decorated a guest room so that the lady would feel at home. They did everything they knew to do to ensure that whoever came would feel the love of Jesus.

No one came. Even though there were many ladies in that situation locally, each chose to stay somewhere else. After about a year they withdrew their offer and turned that room into a home office, perplexed at the Lord's reaction to their offer of ministry.

What happened? We'll never know. But there is something we can learn from such "unanswered prayer"—how to approach the disappointment.

There are a number of negative things we can say about Jonah: He didn't love his enemy the Ninevites. He didn't surrender to God's will even as he was doing what the Lord wanted him to do. And in the end he was angry that the Lord showed grace to his enemy. But, for all that, there's an overriding, positive aspect of his life and his relationship with God that we should emulate.

For Jonah, God was real.

As real as the boat that carried him away and the great fish that dragged him back. As real as the Ninevites he was sent to save. As real as the vine that gave him shade and as real as the worm that devoured it. God was a real character in the story of his life. When he prayed, he prayed to someone he knew intimately. When he ran, he was running from someone real. And he knew the God he prayed to and ran from—knew his grace, his persistence, his justice, his love, and his discipline.

Is God real to you? Is he standing in the room with you right now?

Or when you pray are you just hoping someone might overhear you—that if all the rumors about God are true, he might give a listen to your request?

We are finite human beings, and God is an infinite and an infinitely complex God. For us to understand all the subtleties of our relationship with him would be impossible. But one thing we must know absolutely: God exists. *He is.* Jesus exists; he is at the Father's right hand, interceding for us. And the Holy Spirit exists; he is applying God's plan of salvation to the world. When we see that God is as real as this book you're now reading, as real as the chair you sit on or the car you drive, then praying to him becomes real also.

Then prayer is no longer just words whispered to the wind, or a ritual before dinner, or something you do at church. It becomes communication to a God you know is there, a God who loves you personally. You ask him for things with the knowledge that he will answer—not as you might expect, perhaps, but you know he's listening and acting upon your requests. He becomes an important character in your own life, a wealthy, omnipotent, omniscient parent.

It was a real God who said no to Calli and her husband. For whatever reason, it was a real person who knew what was best for them and was accomplishing his purpose in their lives. Knowing that softens, then dissolves, the disappointment. Calli still wonders why he said no, but she never doubts it was the best reply she could have gotten.

But just as a reply of "no" might be frustrating, a reply of "yes" might be terrifying—the mountains might actually move!

MOUNTAINS MIGHT MOVE

I have a dear friend who sold items costing large corporations millions of dollars. It was not only a career to him, but also, like my work as a probation officer, a kind of day job. He had a gift that he used for the Lord, and it gave him a ministry he loved. He longed to be able to spend more time using his gift. So he prayed that sometime in the next few years he would find a job where he could pay the bills, work out of his home, and have more time free to serve the Lord.

Almost immediately negative things started happening at work. Large corporate accounts he'd had for years suddenly decided to do business with his competition. People who worked at his company's headquarters and had supported his sales efforts suddenly quit, making his job very difficult. Large sales he and his management had been counting on either dried up or also went to his competition. Within months his career turned sour. His territory was cut, then, when things continued to go bad, he was fired.

Since his wife was working and he had his retirement savings to live on, they had enough money to last about ten months. He started looking for a job in his career specialty. No jobs were available. He then started looking for any job in sales. No one would hire him. The months clicked away, as did their savings. Both he and his wife became anxious. He looked harder, even contacted headhunters and got them looking. When none of that bore fruit, he tried various home crafts in the hope that one of them might catch on and start generating income. None did.

The tenth month arrived, and they faced having to live on his wife's salary, which meant losing one of the cars, the house—just about everything but the essentials. Winds of panic were beginning to blow, and they blew in a dark sense of bitterness. God was finally going to let him down.

That's when a cousin who lived in Tennessee called. The cousin had just heard my friend was out of work, and he told him about a job that was his for the asking. It was a job he would never have considered before, but now it looked like it might just save them. There was a concern, though: it paid his cousin's bills in Tennessee, but would it generate enough income to pay much higher bills in Southern California? But, since it was the only thing around, my friend took it.

It not only has paid the bills for about six years now, but he's working from his house, and he's able to spend much more time in ministry.

He's lost a career, but gained more time for the Lord.

God is real. He is in the room with you right now. What do you want to ask him?

I have a dear little granddaughter who visits me as often as she can. Sometimes when she's over in the evening, I have work that I have to complete, so I sit in my easy chair and keep busy while she and her grandmother enjoy each other's company. Sometimes she wants to include me in what's going on, so she'll call to me from only a few feet away: "Grandpa." I love the sound of that word. But at that moment my concentration blocks out her sweet little voice, and I don't hear her.

"He's not listening," she'll say to her grandmother, and my lovely wife tells her to go over to me and tug on my sleeve. That always does the trick.

When I don't respond the first time, she doesn't say, "Grandpa doesn't exist, does he?" or "Grandpa doesn't love me; he wouldn't do what I want anyway," or "Grandpa never listens." No. She knew I was there; she just had to get my attention first. In the same way, we know God is there. And we don't have to get God's attention. He always hears you the first time you call.

So when you pray, be prepared for an answer. It will be a loving answer, perhaps taking you through some anxious moments, but when all is said and done, you'll see the primary thing the Lord is trying to teach you: you can, and should, completely trust in him.

A CASE OF TRUST

When one of my boys was three years old, he was diagnosed as having polio. You can imagine how hard this hit the family, particularly his mother and me. Fortunately, he was too young to understand what was happening to him. In desperation, we asked for a second opinion. He indeed had polio. In fact, the physical damage was already beginning: his left leg was showing signs of withering.

I called the elders of the church together, and we laid hands on him and prayed over him. On the next visit to the doctor, he could see no signs of the disease. The polio was gone.

The Lord left a huge impression on me: he was there, right there with us, not only for me but for my whole family.

Why did he allow the disease, then heal it through prayer?

I believe it was because of our weakness and unbelief. Those of us who are blessed to be in the Lord's service, particularly where there is danger and frustration, need to be reminded now and again that the Lord is right there with us. We need to be reminded that he is a mighty God, able to calm any storm our leaky little boats may head into. Otherwise our sinful natures would soon lose sight of him.

Miracles like this—and the five thousand dollars, and the hole in the ground—keep him right before us where he belongs. They continually teach us that we can trust in him, completely, totally, without exception.

Perhaps the more anxious the moments he takes us through, the darker the shadows in the valley, the deeper the impression he's trying to make on us. So we end up saying, "If he took us through that, he'll take us through this."

Are you burdened for the inner city? Do you have a gift you want to share, but you don't know how? Go to the Lord in prayer. Seek his guidance and leading. Then go where he leads. Get involved in the way and at the level he provides. And trust that all will work together for your, and your ministry's, good.

And may I be the first to thank you for your efforts.

Now let's continue by looking at some of the ministries you might find within the inner city.

CHAPTER 10

But What CAN I DO?

Now Nineveh was an exceedingly great city, a three-day journey in extent. And Jonah began to enter the city on the first day's walk. Then he cried out and said, "Yet forty days, and Nineveh shall be overthrown!"

Jonah 3:3–4

Jonah was given a very well-defined task. His message was clear and concise, his route well laid out, even the duration of the project was set. I believe the Lord knew that if he gave his hesitant prophet any leeway at all, he would find a way to wiggle out of the job. So the Lord gave him very specific instructions.

Our job description, however, is not so specific. We have a broad outline of the task in the form of the Great Commission:

And Jesus came and spoke to them, saying, "All authority has been given to Me in heaven and on earth. Go therefore and make disciples of all the nations, baptizing them in the name of the Father and of the Son and of the Holy Spirit, teaching them to observe all things that I have commanded you; and lo, I am with you always, even to the end of the age." (Matt. 28:18–20)

167

Because the Great Commission leaves us on our own to figure out the details, the types and forms of ministry are as varied as the imaginations of God's people—and God himself. Ministry includes just about anything that shares the gospel of Jesus Christ with sinners—which is what we all were before we came to know him.

Even something as simple as a hobby can turn into an opportunity for ministry, as the following example shows.

Mrs. Herman loved to cultivate African violets. Her windowsills were lined with them, all sorts of delicate colors and varieties. As is true of many of our seasoned citizens, she was an early riser, and she abhorred violence. So when anyone in her neighborhood experienced violence, particularly the death of a loved one, she would rise early and, before the neighborhood began to stir, place an African violet at his or her front door. Stuck in the potting soil was a small, elegantly fashioned sign: "My prayers of comfort are with you. In Jesus' name, Mrs. Herman." Often the recipients would stop by to thank her, giving an opportunity for a gentle, loving witness. Mrs. Herman's hobby became her ministry.

Other types of informal, unstructured ministry are the special projects prompted by holidays or special needs. One man's simple idea for collecting free turkeys is a perfect example.

GABE AND THE THANKSGIVING TURKEYS

Gabe is a member of a church that has about three hundred attendees on Sunday morning. Not a large church, but not small either. Gabe is not one to initiate things.

He has ideas for ministry, but he usually talks himself out of following through on them. But Thanksgiving was approaching, and an idea struck that just wouldn't go away.

His idea concerned the holiday promotions at the local supermarkets:

"Spend $100 on groceries and get a free turkey."

"Spend $25 and get a turkey for 19¢ a pound."

"Buy one turkey, get another one free."

There were others, but they all added up to free or cheap turkeys.

In the past Gabe had been involved with a rescue mission downtown. He had given the message there periodically, but hadn't done that in a long time. Yet he was still concerned about those men, and the families that came for food on the holidays.

If he could enlist the people of the church, Gabe realized, those interested could buy their own turkeys and donate the free or cheap turkey to the rescue mission. He would even pick them up and deliver them, making it as easy as possible on the contributors.

Getting permission from the pastor, Gabe put together a small flyer and put it on the pews Sunday morning. People started calling. The first week about ten responded, the next week about twice that. By Thanksgiving, his idea had resulted in forty-three turkeys for the mission. They fed one thousand people and gave out another thousand food baskets; Gabe's turkeys helped.

Gabe's reward came one afternoon when he was delivering some of the turkeys. He pulled up to the front of the mission, knocked on the door, and quickly transferred the turkeys to a waiting worker. Returning to his car, he passed a young Hispanic man standing there with a small child in a stroller. "God bless you, sir," the man called out.

Gabe turned, a little surprised that anyone would thank him for what he was doing. "God bless you too," he replied.

Like Gabe, or like my friend who collected warm clothing for the snowbound Navajo, you may have an idea for a onetime project or an occasional ministry.

However, when we think of ministries that we can plug into, we usually think of formal ones—ones with budgets—that can use help at several skill levels. I want to share some examples of these types of ministries and give you some ideas for starting your own outreach, as well as the names of some established ministries you can contact for more information.

CHILD CARE

The inner city has more than its share of broken homes, far more than its share of single mothers. Often, in order to earn a living, these mothers need child-care facilities they can trust. One of the first outreach ministries at St. Stephen's was a licensed child-care facility. It gave us the opportunity to witness to both the child and the mother. There's nothing that shows you care more for the mother than to show you truly care for her child.

As with any ministry, there are a lot of misses—the road to destruction is wide with a lot of feet shuffling down it. But there were some hits too. Carla's mom, for example.

Carla was four. A sweet little lady with an infectious smile that covered her whole face, a sly, beyond-her-years tilt to her mouth, and wide, exploring eyes. And nothing seemed to scare her either. The moment she arrived, Carla plunged right in doing the things we give kids her age to do: coloring, working puzzles, making things with rubber stamps, singing—especially singing. We find children learn about Jesus more quickly when they sing about him. And since we have a good tape library of Christian music for children, we play a lot of it during the day.

Her mother, Bambi, had little Carla before marriage and high school graduation. Even though Bambi could have finished school, she decided to go to work. She found a job in a florist's shop doing general clean-up and sometimes, when the owner and workers were particularly busy, making up some of the easier flower arrangements. She quickly found that she was fascinated by flower arranging. She had seen professionally arranged flowers before, of course, but she had never seen the arrangements come together. "It was neat. I'd see them start with a single color, then add others, then take away a color and add another. Then more greens and whites. I even started to learn the names of the flowers." After arranging simple bouquets for a while, she became more creative; her eyes and fingers were always eager to learn more.

It was an exciting time for Bambi. Neither of her parents ever encouraged their kids, so she had grown up believing she had little to offer. She had dropped out of school primarily because she saw it as a waste of time; she had no particular skills to build upon. Now she not only had a skill, but an artistic one—one that allowed her to bring beauty to her life, and other lives as well. She found something new in herself when she

171

woke in the morning: hope for the future and the future of her child.

Summer gave way to autumn and more often than not the skies were overcast, a prelude to rain. One of those bleak, rainy mornings the owner of the shop called her into his back office and made her morning even bleaker. His teenage daughter had suddenly decided she wanted to work in her daddy's store, a dream he'd had for years. The only position open to her was Bambi's. "Sorry, but you understand—or you will someday." He fired her. Bambi was out.

The world a horribly hostile place again, Bambi picked up little Carla at the day-care center. Although she tried to keep Carla from seeing the pain, it was impossible. Tears crowded the edges of her eyes, and her heart seemed to empty of all good things. But she managed to remain dry-eyed as she walked Carla most of the way home.

About a block away, Carla began to sing, "Jesus loves me, this I know." When she got to the part that said, "Little ones to him belong; they are weak but he is strong," Bambi began to cry. She was no child, but she needed someone to help her, someone to keep her afloat in a very stormy sea. She needed the Jesus of Carla's song.

Knowing she was actually walking away from the one place she might find him, Bambi turned and retraced her steps to the church. She and I talked for a while about Jesus, and a few weeks later, after attending our church faithfully, Bambi was saved.

As it turned out, the shop owner and his daughter could not get along. The young woman exploded one day and quit in a huff. After the owner assured Bambi that she wouldn't be replaced quite so easily again, she returned to creating beautiful floral arrangements. Jesus does love her—the Bible tells her so—and we had the opportunity to minister that love to her because her daughter was in our day-care center.

Ministry Opportunities
Child Care

Ministries to children not only help the child, they serve as an outreach to the child's parents. Here are some ideas for helping a church-sponsored day-care center or other child-care facility.

- collect toys appropriate for toddlers
- provide consumable materials like paper, pencils, crayons, and coloring books
- gather Christian books for children, also audio- and videotapes
- help make the classrooms eye-catching by painting, room design, or graphics
- volunteer to read to the children or assist in the classroom
- assemble and/or create learning materials
- help create and produce brochures, announcements, mailers, and other publicity materials
- offer administrative assistance in the office

CHRISTIAN SCHOOLS

We saw early on the ministry potential in childhood education. With our K–12 school, as with the day-care program, we are ministering to both children and parents—perhaps more to the parents. Those who are willing to pay for a Christian education, even if they're not already Christians, at least see the merit in the Christian life and are often interested in discussing it. And, since we also have scholarships available for parents who are financially pressed, we touch the whole community.

None were quite so pressed, financially, emotionally, and psychologically, as twelve-year-old Charlotte.

Police suspected her father of being in a gang and dealing drugs. One night they decided to raid the house. So their suspect wouldn't have time to flush the evidence, they burst through the front door. As mother and daughter screamed, the cops grabbed the father, planted him spread-eagle facing the wall, and started patting him down. Charlotte cowered in the corner, her eyes glued on what was happening.

Just when they had finished assuring themselves he was unarmed, it happened: a white officer, gun drawn, pushed through the front door; as the other officers watched dumbfounded, he pumped two bullets into the father's back, murdering him.

I was asked to do the funeral and decided to give Charlotte a full scholarship to St. Stephen's. Although it was rough going in the beginning, Charlotte worked hard. She didn't have to think when she was working, and she had more than just her father's death to think about. Her mother began leaving Charlotte alone—first at night, then for days at a time. When Charlotte told her teachers about it, we spoke to her mother, but it did no good. Soon her mother abandoned her altogether.

We went to court and had Charlotte placed with one of our church families. Although that was a temporary solution to her family problems, the permanent solution came when she accepted Jesus Christ as her personal Lord and Savior. Charlotte made it through school with flying colors, got a job with FedEx right after graduation, and is now married and expecting her first child.

Our K–12 is like most others. We teach what needs to be taught. But we also love our children. Not a permissive love, but a strong, enduring love, that can, and often does, shepherd them through some difficult times and over some extremely high hurdles.

One of the ways we love our kids is to see them as God's people, even when others might see them as a little strange.

Arnold came to us in his early teens. His parents thought him a very difficult case—maybe even mentally deranged. Arnold liked to draw. That in itself isn't all that strange, but what he liked to draw was macabre. Dead people. Corpses. And caskets, all sorts of caskets. Plain caskets. Ornate ones. Sometimes they were open with the bodies inside, the faces etched in death.

We decided the best approach with Arnold was to get to know him, since he wasn't hurting anyone and was otherwise a reasonable youngster. We soon found out that what he was doing wasn't strange at all, to his way of thinking at any rate. From a very early age Arnold had wanted to be a mortician. Upon learning this, we decided to help him along. I knew of a Christian mortician in the city and invited him to speak to the students. We made sure that he and Arnold met. Arnold, of course, was thrilled.

In his senior year, Arnold went to work for the mortician, and, during that year, confirmed his reliance on Jesus as his Savior and Lord. Then he was off to the

University of Illinois to study business. Upon completion of his business degree, he studied mortuary sciences. When he graduated, he came back to work for the local mortician, saved his money, and bought a "dying" mortuary in Oakland, California. Within a few years he had turned it into a thriving business. The last time I saw Arnold, he drove up in his Mercedes and thanked us for our understanding. He now provides scholarships for youngsters like Charlotte.

Most of the time parents are the ones who place their children at St. Stephen's, but one time a sixteen-year-old student enrolled himself. Chuck's father had been living what charitably could be called a sinful life—drinking, gambling, doing drugs, carousing with women. Not only did he live this way, but he reveled in it.

Until, that is, he got hold of one of our tracts and started attending St. Stephen's. When he was saved, everything changed. Now he was home at night, interested in what Chuck was doing in school, lovingly disciplining his son, talking to him about things that mattered. Chuck decided that if Christians were able to accomplish this change in his father, he wanted to be around Christians. He enrolled at St. Stephen's.

The ultimate goal in our Christian school, beyond providing a solid education, is to share the gospel. So when I suggest that you get involved in a Christian school by doing something like tutoring, it's really two jobs: to help the child in a particular subject, and to develop a sound enough relationship with the child to be able to share Christ. If the child is already a Christian, then you have the opportunity to further the kingdom by strengthening the child emotionally as well as intellectually.

Ministry Opportunities
K–12 School

Every inner-city Christian school is working under-staffed and on a shoestring budget. There are always things you can do, starting with the same suggestions listed under Child Care. Here are some other ideas:

- establish mentoring relationships
- donate school supplies (ask for a grade-specific list)
- tutor kids in math, science, or computer skills
- tutor kids in the arts—music, painting, crafts
- tutor kids in language skills—reading and writing
- assist a teacher in the classroom once a week
- help coordinate a field trip or chaperon an event
- enlist a business to sponsor a sports team by providing equipment and uniforms
- donate (or encourage others to donate) class-room equipment: overhead projectors and audiovisual equipment, for example
- help with fund-raising projects: bake sales, craft fairs, recycling drives, etc.
- mentor a child by spending one hour each week teaching him or her life skills
- provide expertise for topic-specific support groups dealing with substance abuse, domes-tic violence, or other issues
- plan work-study opportunities

ST. STEPHEN'S
RETIREMENT CENTER

At the other end of the spectrum from our childhood education ministry is our retirement center. Sixty apartments house active seniors from age sixty-two to ninety-five. Only 20 percent of them have attended our church, which means that 80 percent are new to us. Some are even new to the Lord. As an outreach ministry, there are Bible studies and spiritual activities, and the residents are encouraged to attend church with us.

But we also bring the church to them with our Adopt-a-Senior program. Members of our church become their friends, help them when needed, visit them, and generally keep them cheered. Most are able to take care of themselves, since this is an active senior center. But sometimes they get a little under the weather like the rest of us. When that happens, their adoptive families supply them with hot meals, clean their apartments, and take care of their basic needs. Our desire is to show our senior citizens the love of Christ—they'll be encouraged if they do know him, or we'll give them the opportunity to come to know him through us.

Ministry Opportunities
Retirement Center or Nursing Home

Most residents of a retirement center or nursing home never receive a visit from family or friends. Their loneliness is a wonderful opportunity for Christians to practice the golden rule: If you were

---

an elderly person not able to see your family whenever you wanted, what would you like done?

- visit the residents just to talk or play games
- read Scripture to them (many with failing eyesight can no longer read their Bibles)
- provide reading materials—magazines and books, especially large-print editions
- donate videotapes
- help residents decorate their rooms by hanging pictures, curtains, etc.
- provide flowers for those who are ill
- work outdoors—many seniors love to garden but need help with the heavier work
- when you can't visit, write them a note or send a card
- teach a class in arts and crafts, or provide the materials for one
- encourage them and help them face the passing of friends and loved ones

SKILLS FOR LIVING

Like child care, as various needs were identified by our congregation, ministries rose up to meet them. Currently at St. Stephen's, and I'm sure at other inner-city churches, we have a counseling center that ministers to those who abuse drugs and other substances, those who need housing or medical referrals, those who need HIV-AIDS counseling, or marriage and pre-marital counseling, those who need assistance managing their personal finances, and those who require vocational and career placement.

Although when listed they seem so sterile and formal, each ministry was born when real people came to St. Stephen's desperate for help. Our job, therefore, is to show each one who comes how knowing Christ leads to a satisfied life.

Since we have the counseling center and many in the congregation have been touched by it, the congregation itself has often risen to the counseling needs of the community. Here is a good example.

Carol was a single parent. Her daughter, Millie, was thirteen. Carol met Terrance at a local party and after they had dated for a while, he moved in with Carol and Millie. Terrance worked at an auto wrecking yard, but he was not a hard worker. He often called in sick and spent those days at home. Carol actually found this a blessing, because Terrance was there when Millie got home from school and could keep an eye on her.

After about a month, though, that blessing became a nightmare. Millie showed up after school at Carol's work. She was close to tears and refused to go home. When pressed, Millie broke down sobbing and told her mother that Terrance had been sexually molesting her, and she just couldn't take it anymore.

As you can imagine, Carol was both devastated and furious; tornadoes of guilt, betrayal, and maternal protection swirled around inside of her. After telling Millie to go to a friend's house, Carol decided to take care of Terrance. She grabbed a gun that the owner of the business kept in his office and went out to find Terrance. As it turned out, he had gone to work that day. Although she knew approximately where the wrecking yard was, she didn't know the precise location.

So when she got into the general area, she got lost. Before long she was driving from this street to that, not even knowing which direction she was going. She saw a woman out in front of her home watering flowers and pulled over to ask directions. The gardener was a member of my congregation, a retiree who loved flowers, but loved people more. "You look so upset, my dear," she said, without answering Carol's question.

"I am. I need to find that wrecking place. Do you know where it is? Right now I'd just like to find the highway again. You must know where the highway is."

"I do. And I'll tell you. But first I want you to come in and have a cup of coffee or tea. It's not good to be so upset while you're driving. You may never get to the wrecking yard."

Carol told me later that she was both annoyed with this woman for delaying her and grateful, for she knew the woman was right. She had nearly hit two parked cars and would probably have ended up as someone's hood ornament if she hadn't calmed down. But the real reason she wanted to calm down was so she'd have a steady hand. She wanted to put a bullet right between Terrance's eyes.

After staring into the depths of the black coffee for a moment or two, Carol began to cry. My church member said later that as she talked to Carol, she could feel the Spirit right there in the room, helping her to choose the right words and warming the hand she finally placed on Carol's. Before long Carol allowed the woman to drive her to our church. An hour later, Carol was praying for salvation in my office.

When Terrance got home that night, Carol did confront him—with the gospel. The surgical light of Jesus pierced Terrance's heart, and he confessed his terrible crime against Millie. Carol brought Terrance to my office that evening and he, too, came to know Jesus. With Carol in the room, Terrance told Millie how terrible his sin had been and asked her forgiveness. That did not come until a few months later, when Millie came to know Jesus, and even then it took years for Millie to completely forgive. No formal charges were brought against Terrance because he went into long and intense counseling. He is now living as a strong witness for Christ. Carol has since married a good Christian man who loves and cares deeply for his new family. He has adopted Millie, who couldn't be happier.

I love stories that end like that. I also love that our congregation has become an effective arm of our counseling center.

Another important aspect of this outreach is job and career counseling. One of the worst things about the current welfare system is that it promotes idleness, and when a person is idle, there's no limit to the mischief he or she can get into. Welfare also promotes an emptiness of spirit.

We were created by God for work. In the Garden we were told to work. The Lord could just as easily have created us for leisure, but he didn't. Right after he packed the meat on our bones, he gave us useful things to do: take care of his creation, be stewards of it, and subdue it for our use. We gain a lot from work— not only our daily provision, but a sense of worth and well-being. The idle lose that, and it's a shame.

BUT WHAT CAN I DO?

At St. Stephen's we promote work and the spiritual and emotional benefits gained from it. In the last six months, through the efforts of our counseling center, we have induced scores of families to leave the welfare rolls and become productive citizens again.

Ministry Opportunities
Parenting Skills and Family Counseling

The strength of any community is in its families. Though the skills needed often overlap with normal adult living skills, some are quite unique to the Christian family. Teaching these skills gives us an important opportunity to share Christ. You might want to share your particular expertise one-on-one, or your Bible study group might want to sponsor a class. Such an effort might include buying all the materials for a class or seminar, including books, workbooks, notebooks, pens, announcements, and publicity materials.

Topics for training classes:
- how to be a Christian father/mother
- biblical discipline of children
- parenting teenagers
- family problem solving
- dealing with a difficult child
- controlling anger
- dealing constructively with differences
- how to be a light in the 'hood
- abortion counseling

Areas of personal involvement:
- mentoring a family
- offering encouragement in times of crisis
- offering advice (legal, financial, parenting) during a crisis
- getting involved in family-issue support groups

Ministry Opportunities
**Assisting Adults or Those with
Adult Responsibilities**

In the inner city we find that even though parents do the best they can, it's often not enough. Many kids are forced to become adults far too soon, or they become adults without ever learning basic skills. Individual or group ministry can provide them with training in the following areas:

- personal hygiene and basic nutrition
- how to deal with medical emergencies
- tips on personal and household security
- specific job counseling
- head-of-household skills: budgeting, paying bills, financial planning, rule making, family management
- home-management skills: cleaning, laundry, sewing, minor home and auto repairs, grocery shopping, bargain hunting

- decision-making skills: weighing alternatives, predicting outcomes, taking responsibility for consequences
- legal issues; avoiding pitfalls
- topic-specific support groups: Parents of Teens, Wives/Husbands of Substance Abusers, Trauma Sufferers (crime victims, especially those who have lost loved ones through violence)
- prayer groups, which meet regularly to pray for specific needs

NEIGHBORHOOD RENEWAL

Not far from our church is a forty-seven-unit apartment complex. It was built in 1987 by absentee landlords, and over the years the management had been lax. Apartments had fallen into disrepair and the grounds had decayed. But, worse by far, the screening process for tenants had also lagged, allowing the gangs to take up residence. They turned four of the units into crack houses and even built trapdoors between the floors to provide an escape route in the event of raids. That made thirty-six crack houses in a ten-block area near the complex.

Decent families were moving out and none were moving in.

The bank was losing ten thousand dollars a month because of the high vacancy rate when they asked us to take over management of the complex in return for a 25 percent interest in the property. A private investment company, Community Development Corporation, agreed to enter into partnership with our church and provide the other 75 percent. Our job was to turn the place around and make it a place decent people would want to live. We decided to do that for Christ.

First, we installed one of our deacons and his wife as managers, definitely a dangerous job. The gangs immediately retaliated, driving by and pumping bullets into the complex. God, of course, was on guard. No one was hurt, and the commitment of our deacon and his wife never faltered.

Next we stopped renting three units, cleaned them up, and turned two of them into a Head Start child-care facility and the other into a prayer room. In that unit we not only held prayer meetings, but we did family, marriage, job, and career counseling.

With the help of others in the church, we started cleaning things up. As part of that effort, we installed a playground able to accommodate about two dozen kids.

Within eighteen months the complex had been turned into a truly pleasant place to live, comfortable and affordable. Most of those thirty-six crack houses in the neighborhood are gone now. We prayed them out of existence!

Access to safe, affordable housing is one of the inner city's greatest problems and offers a special challenge to inner-city ministry. Possibly the most dramatic example of neighborhood renewal comes from Charlotte, North Carolina. And the champion who changed the 'hood there is a woman named Barbara Brewton-Cameron.

Barbara grew up in the Double Oaks neighborhood of Charlotte, identified by the *New York Times* in 1991 as one of the five most violent crime neighborhoods in the U.S. Double Oaks was already well on its way to becoming that in the mid-sixties when Barbara's husband, Casey Brewton, was shot and killed. The murder left her emotionally devastated; it also left her with two young daughters and a son to raise. Barbara left Double Oaks, moved to another part of Charlotte, and did her best to rebuild a life for her family.

In the early seventies, through the ministry of a local evangelist, she came to know the Lord and became active not only in the church, but in the church's outreach to the city's derelict population. By the late seventies, the Lord had convinced Barbara to return to Double Oaks and make a difference in the people's lives there.

When she moved back, she quickly began gathering the neighborhood's children to herself. Using a house (separate from her residence) that cost her two hundred dollars a month to rent—a dear sum for a single woman with three children—she began sharing the love of Jesus with the children who came. Double Oaks was a violent place, plagued by gangs, drugs, shootings. Often she had to get the kids to the floor so they wouldn't be hit by stray bullets. But her work paid off, and soon the parents were becoming involved. And finally, miraculously, Barbara started her own church, Community Outreach Mission Church, on the land next to the little house where she started—a place previously occupied by a "house of ill repute." Among other ministries, this church immediately began working to help those in the neighborhood get off drugs and get on the road to physical and spiritual healing.

As her church began to grow, Barbara, now Pastor Cameron, made contact with Frank Martin, a developer in Charlotte and a Christian who believed he was called to help renew Double Oaks. Barbara, who clearly defined the need, and Frank Martin, who clearly understood what needed to be done, formed a team. Together they convinced the city of Charlotte, the county of Mecklenburg (in which Charlotte resides), law enforcement authorities, and area business and community leaders to adopt Pastor Cameron's vision.

The Charlotte-Mecklenburg Housing Partnership took up the project. Its plan was to buy up homes owned by absentee landlords—those that were the most run-down and housed the gangs and drug dealers—and rehabilitate them. Then they would sell them to first-time home buyers. They turned that neighborhood into Genesis Park, a name Pastor Cameron received from the Lord.

Names are important, and there were two street names within the project that definitely needed changing—Wayt and Kinney. It was known all over the South that if you wanted to buy drugs in Charlotte, you went to Wayt and Kinney. Pastor Cameron felt that was a distinction the project could forgo. So, with great effort, the names of those, and some of the other streets, were changed. Now there's Brewton Drive, Peaceful Way Drive, and Rush Wind Drive.

Not long ago Genesis Park was featured on ABC's *World News Tonight with Peter Jennings* as an example of what could be done within the inner city. (As an aside, there was no mention of the church's contribution.)

About four years ago, Pastor Cameron met Mary Lance Sisk, a member of Forest Hill Church in Charlotte. Mary Lance is known worldwide for her prayer ministry—both teaching about it and being a prayer warrior herself. After what both describe as a heart-stirring meeting where they discussed their dreams for the future, Mary Lance became involved in Pastor Cameron's ministry. The two became cochairs of a new committee whose vision is a Genesis Park Community Center. This is a multipurpose building that will include a full gymnasium, commercial facilities for a soup kitchen operation, as well as a new worship center. This effort not only will further the church ministry, but also will assist other ministries—to the homeless, to substance abusers, and to those transitioning from jails and prisons.

Mary Lance Sisk began to enlist the aid of the Forest Hill Church leadership and members. Those efforts were rewarded when, two years ago, Forest Hill became the sister church of Community Outreach. Together they have become a formidable force for Christ. To break down the barriers we've previously identified, they often hold combined services. They share common goals for ministry and work to achieve them.

Recently, in a show of sacrifice, Forest Hill, a growing church in need of expanded facilities, held a fundraising drive and raised over $400,000 for Community Outreach's building fund. A number of Forest Hill leaders now serve on the building committee at Community Outreach. One of them is Sean Meade, a member of Forest Hill who has committed himself to inner-city ministry through the door opened by Pastor Cameron and Community Outreach. He and his wife, Christine, have moved to Genesis Park so they may become a part of the community with whom they are sharing Christ.

As with any relationship between those with needs and those with resources, there is the danger of the association becoming a paternal relationship, the haves taking care of the have-nots. The two churches work hard to keep that from happening. One way they accomplish this is to focus on what Forest Hill receives in return for their support. The pastor, David Chadwick, puts it this way: "We are privileged to see God working in Community Outreach's ministry and our faith is strengthened that he is also working in our midst, as well."

Ministry Opportunities
Assisting an Inner-City Church

Churches in poor areas are usually poor. Even when the members tithe faithfully, 10 percent of very little is much littler still. As a result, most inner city churches are understaffed and their facilities substandard. There are probably a thousand ways you can help:

- work to maintain or improve the church facilities and grounds
- volunteer as staff or office help
- gather materials and equipment (office supplies and furniture, typewriters, computers)
- locate or refurbish pews and other furniture
- donate hymnals, choral music, or choir robes
- pray consistently for the pastor and staff
- serve as a resource the church can call on for experiential information
- consult on business and financial matters

- establish a computer network; install software
- set up an Inner City Committee of Assistance

An example of what I mean by an Inner City Committee of Assistance (ICCA) is the relationship between Pastor Cameron's church in Charlotte, Community Outreach Mission Church, and Forest Hill Church. It is a group of concerned leadership and members of a suburban church who come together regularly to support a "sister" church in the inner city. With committees made up of members from both churches, the ICCA meets regularly and prayerfully to address specific needs of the inner-city church and to break down any barriers that might exist between the two memberships and communities. Over time, assuming the relationship remains healthy, both sides benefit. The inner-city church receives sorely needed help, and the suburban church gains a greater understanding of what the inner-city church is facing and becomes instrumental in winning many souls for Christ.

MINISTRY TO THE SUFFERING

As I said earlier, when I first told the congregation that we were going to actively minister to those with HIV and AIDS, some members were quite distressed. Could they catch it? What if they sat where an infected person had been sitting? What if someone brushed against an open sore? What about the water in the baptismal pool—could it be contaminated?

And finally, what about the influence those people would have on our children and young adults?

Of course, there were no real answers to these questions. Even if you assured people they were in no danger, how do you really know? And the stakes are high—we're dealing with the lives of our children and our spouses. So I simply told them that the Lord Jesus would protect us as he always had, and if there were any danger, he would see us through it.

But to help set my congregation's fears to rest, we began our ministry by inviting AIDS sufferers to join us at several AIDS forums. By meeting and hearing from some of these men and women, we built a bridge of compassion. A shaky bridge, but one that would at least get us over the initial hurdles. At those forums and through word of mouth we informed the AIDS community that they were welcome to any of our services.

We started prayer meetings for those afflicted with AIDS as well as any other catastrophic illnesses. Many came, and when they did, they heard the unvarnished gospel: faith, trust, and obedience. Since our desire was to destroy the works of the devil, when they came, they found compassion, a nonjudgmental attitude—and Jesus.

San Diego has a Metropolitan Community Church, a homosexual denomination. The news of our ministry spread to that church. One evening their entire congregation attended services, and when I knelt down at the altar to pray, I found the pastor of that church kneeling beside me. I was touched by that event. I may disagree with their interpretation of Scripture, but they, like all of us, are people in need of Christ's love.

As our ministry progressed, people were touched. I've already told you about Stan, but there were others.

One gentleman came to the prayer meeting. While there, the Holy Spirit opened his eyes and he saw hell! Fear gripped his rebellious heart, and he ran home in a frenzy to confront his "roommate." Never having seen him carry on like this, his "roommate" was convinced that he also needed to attend our services. The next Sunday they both came. And at the next midweek prayer meeting, they both accepted Christ's invitation. Both are now married to wonderful women and both have beautiful children.

Clarence's story is unique, the story of a three-year miracle. He suffered from full-blown AIDS. Normally his six-foot frame carried well over two hundred pounds. When I first saw Clarence, he had melted to about 110 pounds and was probably days from death. His mother, also formidable, knelt at the foot of his bed, praying day and night.

One morning her prayers were answered. As a yellow sun broke through half-drawn blinds, Clarence's immune system kicked back on. The doctors confirmed this as he began gaining weight. And with that confirmation his spirits soared. They soared for another reason too. Jesus took up residence in his heart, his mother having helped open that heart. Over the next few weeks Clarence improved and was finally sent home.

Soon after that he met a young lady. After a brief courtship they asked me to marry them. About that time our AIDS ministry had progressed to the point where we had started our own hospice. It had five bedrooms and housed men who wanted to be surrounded by Christian love during their final days. Clarence and his new wife became the managers of that facility.

For the next three years Clarence shared the gospel and the love of Christ with the men who passed through the hospice. Through Clarence's witness, some came to know Christ before they died.

Sadly, Clarence's reprieve was not permanent; after three years in remission the AIDS returned. Soon Clarence was whisked to his Savior's side, having served Jesus faithfully for all the extra time the Lord had given him.

Our AIDS ministry continues. Tragically, many have perished in their sins, but happily, many have been brought to Christ. But there has been another spiritual benefit. Our church is now united around this ministry. Suspicion has turned to love, discomfort to compassion. Those who were against it are now some of its strongest supporters. We are all sinners in need of a Savior—all of us.

MINISTRY TO THE HOMELESS

If there's one ministry that can benefit from outside assistance, it's helping the homeless.

We are involved with a local rescue mission, Victory Outreach, and the Salvation Army. At the rescue mission we provide the service once a week. Then every Wednesday we set up downtown and feed three hundred to five hundred people. We also pass out tracts and attempt to build relationships, which we call upon later in the week, when we come by with a van and collect those who want to attend church. From 10 P.M.

Friday to 2 A.M. Saturday we share the gospel and pray with them. Then we give them a warm bed to sleep on and a hot breakfast when they wake. Those who come to church Sunday morning receive lunch afterward.

We also have a thrift store that supplies the homeless with free shoes and clothing.

Over the years many people have been touched by this ministry, too many to count. When Jesus is in your heart, you carry your home with you.

The true testimonial to this outreach came one night when a homeless couple attended our Saturday night ministry. Instead of staying to the end, they got up about midnight and made for the door.

"Where are you going?" I asked. "It's far warmer in here."

"I know," the man said. "That's why we're going out there to minister to the homeless."

They both gave us a huge smile and headed out to bring the kingdom to those in need.

Ministry Opportunities
Community Assistance

For many of the inner city's needs, especially working with the homeless or with AIDS patients, it's best to initially work through an existing ministry. But you can always suggest new things to make it work better, or you can provide the resources necessary to sustain an ongoing ministry.

Here are some ways you might be able to help an entire community:

- assist a neighborhood watch program or other crime prevention efforts

---

- help with a food bank or other distribution programs: collect food donations, deliver meals, serve in a soup kitchen, witness to participants
- teach gardening and landscaping to beautify the 'hood
- teach arts and crafts to beautify homes
- upgrade playground equipment and clean up parks
- work in a crisis pregnancy center: office work, client counseling, placement
- work in a thrift store: gather clothing and other donations, mark merchandise, help customers
- teach job skills: interview, prepare a résumé, coordinate a business wardrobe
- distribute tracts
- prepare information and/or community newsletters
- support a battered women's or runaway children's shelter through counseling, fund-raising, providing clothes and personal items
- work on an organized renovation project to build or improve housing

CHRIST IN PRISON

When we minister to the homeless, or to those with AIDS, or to those with any other need, we do it out of love for Christ. Matthew 25:35–36 records these words of Jesus: "For I was hungry and you gave Me food; I was thirsty and you gave Me drink; I was a stranger and you took Me in; I was naked and you clothed Me; I was sick and you visited Me; I was in prison and you came to Me."

And that brings me to the last ministry opportunity I want to share with you: ministry to those in prison.

Prison ministries are an awesome responsibility. The men and women in prisons have not only ventured to the edge of a very deep cliff, often they continue to stroll precariously along the edge. A fatal slip could mean an eternity in hell, and there are plenty of folks around willing to give them a little shove. Our message of the gospel is always important, but even more so where life seems so cheap.

A perfect example of being rescued from the edge is Larry, the man who helped launch St. Stephen's ministry to the homeless. Here's his story.

The headline in the *San Diego Daily Transcript* blazes: "Larry Price Rises From Mean Streets To Dispense Hope." In the 1970s Larry was a businessman, an entrepreneur. He and his employees sold drugs from Imperial Beach in San Diego to Oakland, over four hundred miles to the north. Reaping the rewards, Larry lived the high life: expensive house and clothes, cruising the city streets in a fully loaded Cadillac. When his first daughter was born, he heaped her bedroom in cash and let her roll in it.

Not long afterward, beheaded by the same sword he lived by—heroin and cocaine—Larry ended up penniless and on the streets. He survived there for seventeen years, until it all ended with a sentence for burglary. God had brought him to prison so that Larry might meet him there.

But Larry wasn't all that keen on meeting God face-to-face. He just wanted to use God a little. "At first I figured I'd become a Bible-thumper because I thought the parole board might shorten my sentence. It didn't work."

God won't be used, as Larry found out. But he will use us.

"After four years of pretending to be a Christian," Larry goes on, "I actually became one."

When Larry returned to the streets it was as a new Christian on fire for the Lord. And his fire blazed in a furnace whose thermostat was set on *service*. Within the next few months he was helping other ex-cons get jobs. Then he started his own landscaping business and with the help of St. Stephen's landed his first contract. As the business grew, Larry decided to begin his ministry to the homeless. Then, in a dual effort to help clean up the downtown area as well as help teens, he started a nonprofit organization that goes after graffiti. The company currently employs six young people.

Ron is another man who came out of prison and launched into ministry. One of twelve children, nine boys and three girls, Ron was the sixth child; he was born in 1957. He remembers being baptized at about four, too young to know what it signified. Though his mother was not a faithful churchgoer, she wanted her kids to go. But it was Ron's aunt, a faithful Christian, who actually picked them up and took them. When Ron was nine, his aunt passed away. Without her efforts, he and the other kids drifted away from the Lord.

Although Ron stopped going to church, he continued his moral development by attending Archie Moore's ABC Club, which taught moral, spiritual, and physical self-defense. He learned two things there:

- All of the flowers of all the tomorrows are in the seeds of today.

- Even the humblest worker, when moved by the Holy Spirit, touches invisible chords that vibrate and make melodies throughout the eternal ages.

In the late sixties and early seventies, he struggled with his identity and sense of purpose. As with all of us, Ron wanted to be loved and accepted, but, lacking a firm spiritual foundation, his struggle took a destructive turn. He became easily manipulated by men eager to gain his following through lies. He became hateful—vengeful—rebellious toward society as a whole. And he saw the white man as the devil. At age thirteen he began robbing white people's homes in his neighborhood; with the money he stole, he experimented with drugs. Drugs quickly became a way of life.

In December 1972, when he was fifteen, Ron was arrested for armed robbery while still in the store he was burglarizing. He served twenty months with the California Youth Authority (CYA). Occasionally churches would come to minister, but he wasn't falling for any of that. Whitey was the devil and Jesus had blond hair and blue eyes. In August of 1974, then seventeen, he came back from the CYA. He was bigger and more educated, but he was still firmly in rebellion.

He was good at sports, so when he got out of jail again he was recruited by a number of universities for baseball and football. But going away to school would mean leaving familiar surroundings. He decided instead to go to a junior college. Displaying a difficult attitude toward other students got him intentionally injured on the football practice field. In pain for both the physical and emotional injury, Ron's hatred grew. In 1975 he turned his back on education and, indeed, on society; he committed himself to a life of drugs and crime. Ron joined others and together they burglarized homes from La Jolla to San Ysidro. In January 1976, scarcely a few months after leaving school, he and thirteen others made history. They were arrested for perpetrating the biggest ring of home robberies ever in San Diego.

Released from jail in November 1976, he returned to drugs—this time PCP. It landed him in the county mental health facility more than once as he struggled to reestablish his mental stability: he would hear voices and be overwhelmed by bouts of fear. During this intense battle he longed for the time when he felt close to God. Two women came into his life (one he knew from an early age), both Christians. They prayed for him and took him to church. They showed him true Christian love, looking beyond his faults to what he could be in Christ. But the PCP-induced voices remained, and he kept doing drugs.

It was as if this brief brush with Christianity had alerted Satan. *This one is not going to get away,* Satan probably vowed. Although we cannot release Ron from his responsibility, it was as if Satan now submerged Ron in more and more drugs. It no longer mattered what the drug was; if it was in front of him, he took it. For the next few years Ron would come back to the Lord, but then fall away, each time to what seemed like an even more destructive life.

The best example might be the last. On the first Sunday of 1988, Ron came to church and asked for deliverance from the drugs and from everything that tied him to that horrible life. For the next four days he was sober, and then he met a friend from the old days. Within two weeks he was arrested, this time for seventeen counts of robbery and two kidnap–robberies. The two kidnapping counts each carried a twenty-five-year prison term.

God had gotten his attention.

Ron began reading and seeking him. Two devotionals became daily reading, *The Days of Praise* and *Daily Bread.* One of the devotions was titled, "Deliverance for Those Who Are Bound by Sin." Ron suddenly saw his arrest as an act of God's grace. A grace that continued. Instead of getting fifty years, he got eight, of which he served four and a half years. And instead of going to *do* time, God sent him there to *invest* his time—in Jesus. He became part of one of our growing fellowships in prison, and while there he gave his heart and soul to the Lord Jesus. The Lord blessed him in many ways, including one he had no right to expect.

A friend on the outside suggested he begin writing to a young lady, Theresa, and they quickly became pen pals. When he still had eighteen months to go, she came to visit him. She must have made quite an impression because the day he got out of prison, March 4, 1992, he married her.

Ron has never looked back, although he's gone back. He's currently on our staff at St. Stephen's, sharing the good news of Jesus Christ to others in that same prison. With a burden for drug addicts, prisoners, and hurting souls, he holds Bible studies in the prison facilities, at honor camps, and at the San Diego Rescue

Mission. He is also active at our "reentry" house where ex-prisoners come for assistance in readjusting to life on the outside.

None of those he works with can accuse Ron of not knowing what they are going through. He's been through it all.

Another one who has been through it all is Raymond. Like Ron, Raymond did his first stretch at the CYA at age thirteen. After that he was in and out of correctional facilities until he ended up doing a four-year stint at the R. J. Donovan Correctional Facility in San Diego. We had the privilege of bringing him the gospel, and Raymond was saved. "Now I have the privilege of going back into that same prison to express the redeeming power of our Lord and Savior Jesus Christ," he says. "I no longer have to prove my manhood by being a criminal. I am much more a man by living for Christ as a husband and the father of two lovely daughters."

God faithfully takes us where we have to go, then he meets us there and brings us forth—from darkness to sunlight—to meet and minister to others so that we might help them on that same magnificent journey.

In the preceding chapters we've often seen definite results from ministry, both ours and others. Those results may not be what we wanted, but they were at least conclusive. Often, however, the results we see are not so easily identified. Or, perhaps, clearly identifiable results suddenly turn murky, even heartbreaking. In an effort to prepare you for what you might experience in your own ministry, in the next chapter I'd like to share something about trusting the results to God.

How to Locate Inner-City Ministries Near You

What follows is a brief list of inner-city ministries in a few of the larger metropolitan areas. If you live in or near any of them, these ministries are a good place to start. If none of these are close to you, here are a few ideas to help you locate an inner-city ministry nearby:

- If you attend a church from a large denomination, contact your home missions board and ask them about inner-city churches in a metropolitan area near you.
- If you belong to an independent church, ask your pastor if he knows a colleague in the inner city.
- Or, you can call the closest Church of God in Christ (the largest black Pentecostal denomination) and ask them how you might help.
- Contact the Salvation Army or your local rescue mission.

Pastor Robert I. Winley
Soul Saving Station
P.O. Box 200
New York, NY 10027
(212) 662-9425

Dr. E. L. Woodside Sr.
First Church of God In Christ
Inner City Ministries
155 Fulton Ave.
Hempstead, NY 11550
(516) 486-2223
(516) 485-5626 FAX

Dr. Chip Murray
First African Methodist Episcopal
2270 S. Harvard Blvd.
Los Angeles, CA 90018
(213) 730-9180

Dr. John M. Perkins
John M. Perkins Foundation
1803 Robinson Street
Jackson, MI 39209
(601) 354-9840 Home
(601) 352-1497 Office
also located in Pasadena:
1581 Navarro Ave.
Pasadena, CA 91103
(626) 798-7431
(626) 798-1816 FAX

Pastor Cecil Williams
Glide Memorial Church
330 Ellis Street
San Francisco, CA 94102
(415) 771-6300

Dr. Donald Green
San Francisco Christian Center
5825-45 Mission Street
San Francisco, CA 94112-4017
(415) 584-5515

Dr. Tony Evans
The Urban Alternative
P.O. Box 4000
Dallas, TX 75208
(214) 943-3868
(214) 941-5493 FAX

Bishop Dwight McDaniels
San Francisco Christian Center
10191 Halls Perry
St. Louis, MO 63136
(314) 388-3300
(314) 388-4383 FAX

Dr. Fred Lofton
Metropolitan Baptist Church
767 Walker Ave.
Memphis, TN 38126
(901) 946-4095 or 948-8311

Dr. Alvin O. Jackson, Senior Pastor
Mississippi Boulevard Christian Church
70 North Bellevue
Memphis, TN 38104
(901) 729-6222
(901) 726-5418 FAX

Rev. Cleflo Dollar
World Changers Ministries
P.O. Box 490124
College Park, GA 30349
(770) 907-9490 or 997-6895

Bishop Eddie Long
New Birth Missionary Baptist Church
2778 Snapfinger Road
Decatur, GA 30034
(770) 981-5594 or 981-9430

Dr. Suzan D. Johnson Cook
Bronx Christian Fellowship
888 Grand Concourse
Bronx, NY 10451
(718) 993-5654
(718) 993-5733 FAX

Pastor Shirley Caesar
Shirley Caesar Ministries
606 West Club Boulevard
Durham, NC 27701
(919) 683-1161
(919) 688-7519 FAX

Bishop George McKinney
St. Stephen's Church of God in Christ
5825 Imperial Ave.
San Diego, CA 92114
(619) 262-2671
(619) 262-8335 FAX

Pastor Barbara Brewton-Cameron
Community Outreach Christian Ministries
1222 Oaklawn Ave.
P.O. Box 16714
Charlotte, NC 28297
(704) 333-4280
(704) 333-4231 FAX

Jerry and David Upton
Inner City Church
3907 Martin Luther King Jr. Blvd.
Knoxville, TN 37914
(423) 546-0310 or 525-4949

Bishop Charles F. Blake
West Angeles Church of God in Christ
3045 Crenshaw Boulevard
Los Angeles, CA 90016
(213) 733-8300
(213) 733-5929 FAX

Pastor Jesse McKinney
St. Stephen's North Church of God in Christ
1354 N. "G" Street
San Bernadino, CA 92405
(909) 885-5140

Dr. Robert Franklin, President
Interdenominational Theological Center
700 Martin Luther King Jr. Drive, S.W.
Atlanta, GA 30314
(404) 527-7700

CHAPTER 11

Trusting
the Results
TO GOD

So Jonah went out of the city and sat on the east side of the
city. There he made himself a shelter and sat under it in the
shade, till he might see what would become of the city.

Jonah 4:5

Jonah saw his brief ministry in Nineveh save over a hundred thousand souls from destruction. He saw it happen quickly—too quickly, for his tastes. When he sat by the east wall of the city, there was no doubt in his mind as to what the Lord had done. That's why he was so gravely disturbed by it. If anyone asked him what the result of his short stint in Nineveh was, he could answer unequivocally: God had done a mighty work and people repented and were saved from destruction—a whole city of people.

But God doesn't always work like that. Too often I find myself sinfully thinking that the Lord leaves a lot of things up in the air. Sometimes he leaves a lot of room for us to wonder what really is going on.

CHRISTMAS AT THE FUNKY GHETTO

There are two holidays I love above all others—Pentecost and Christmas. Maybe because with both of these we are celebrating God coming to earth. Pentecost cheers the coming of the Holy Spirit, the Comforter. His mission here is to apply the gospel of Jesus Christ to the hearts of men and to bring to salvation those whom the Lord has chosen from the foundation of the world. Christmas celebrates the coming to earth of our Redeemer and his birth in a Bethlehem stable.

In 1966 I was so excited that Christmas was coming, I wanted to share my joy with the congregation the first minute I legitimately could. To that end I scheduled a Christmas service for one minute after midnight—the very moment Christmas Eve becomes Christmas morning, with all the promise it holds.

What a glorious service I envisioned it to be.

I pictured the pews filled with joyful Christians. My mind saw candles glowing and heard voices raised in song. I envisioned prayers floating up to the throne, the first prayers from San Diego that the Lord would get that Christmas. How wonderful it would be.

I published the schedule and announced the Christmas service from the pulpit.

When that night arrived, Jean, my wonderful wife, joined me at the door of the church as the minutes ticked away toward midnight. We were poised to welcome the early birds. There were no early birds; there were no birds at all. No one came. My palm was never clasped. There is a Palm Sunday before Easter, but this was the first Palm*less* service at Christmas.

About fifteen minutes after midnight Jean wrapped understanding arms around my neck and gave me a sweet peck on the cheek. "At least we'll get to bed early and be rested for the kids in the morning."

I nodded. But to my surprise I wasn't depressed. If anything, my batteries were even more charged than they had been before. I was bordering on excitement. "What's open this time of night?" I asked Jean.

"Nowhere I'd care to go."

"I know, a bar. What's the name of that bar down the way?" I turned as if I could see through walls. "The Funky Ghetto—isn't that it?"

"Like I said, nowhere I'd care to go."

"Come with me. I want to make a phone call."

Jean followed me into my office. I got the bar's number from information and dialed it. A gruff, weary voice answered.

"Are you the manager?" I asked.

"As close to one as you'll get tonight."

I introduced myself. "I'd like to come down there and celebrate Christmas with you and your patrons— preach a Christmas message."

"You know who you're calling, right?"

"The Funky Ghetto?"

"Yeah." There was a pause, a few quick breaths. I heard some music grinding in the background. "Sure. Why not?"

Jean decided not to go. She could imagine what was going to happen to me about a second after I started preaching, and she didn't want to be part of it.

The Funky Ghetto was a "go-go" bar, a boxy place with a tall sign featuring a scantily clad woman gyrating in passion-pink neon. It was not hard to find. About ten cars were parked in the lot when I pulled up. As I got out of the car I could hear muffled music permeating the wooden walls. After a couple of deep breaths to reassure my sanity, I stepped inside.

The instant I opened the door, the rhythm of the music slapped me in the face. It was so pronounced, I felt like a rug at beating time. The lights were dim and it took my eyes a moment to adjust. Had the sour odor of beer and liquor been replaced by the earthen smell of manure, the place would have probably been very much like that stable in Bethlehem. Everything was wood, deep and dark, and the scattering of tables and chairs gave the place an unkempt look. Of course, the stable would not have had a bar that stretched along the far wall. Nor the two dancers who wiggled on pedestals, as the neon sign outside advertised. Both dancers had very little on, but they were working very hard. The pedestals stood on either side of a small stage; the patrons, scattered at the tables, focused their attention equally on the two ladies.

I walked up to the bartender as if I belonged there.

"I'm Pastor McKinney from St. Stephen's. I called you a few minutes ago."

I was half expecting him to deny that he'd ever heard of me, but instead he smiled warmly and pushed a hand of welcome to me. As I shook it, he said, "You sure you want to do this?"

"Very."

"Okay, Reverend, they're all yours." He walked to a part of the bar closest to the dancers and flipped a couple of wall switches. The lights came on and the music stopped. Instantly the patrons started catcalling; the dancers looked vulnerable and confused, far more childlike than when they were dancing. "Folks, Pastor McKinney has something to say to you."

The moment the word *pastor* was used, one of the dancers, a blonde with visible dark roots, shrank back in embarrassment and ran from the stage.

"Pastor?" someone groaned. "You selling tickets to something?"

"No," I said. "But I do want to tell you about something."

I began to preach. I spoke about Jesus and about what we were celebrating at Christmas. I spoke about his mission and how he accomplished it on the cross. Then I spoke about salvation and what it meant to each of the people there. When it was over, I invited anyone who wanted to speak to me to do so. I said I would be at a table having a glass of water, to wet my cotton mouth, and waited for whoever might come.

As I walked to the bar to get the water, a guy stopped me and thanked me for speaking. I asked if he had any family; he just nodded and thanked me again. He obviously did not want to speak about his family or himself.

Water in hand, I went to the table. By the time I reached it, the lights were dim again and the music was grinding. But this time only one of the ladies was dancing. The other was waiting for me at the table. She was the one who had ducked out when I was introduced. Now she stood there clad in a terry-cloth robe.

"Pastor." Her voice was tentative, self-conscious.

"Sit. Please. What can I help you with, my dear?"

She sat when I did and began telling me her story. She had been raised a Christian, but when she went to college she had slowly fallen away. First with drinking at parties, then with boys, then with pot and a little cocaine. "I hate myself when I do it. I really do. I've been worrying about what was going to happen to me. Then you came in here tonight. It was like God tracking me down and telling me to get my act together. I guess it can't get any worse than the Funky Ghetto, huh?"

"It can get a lot worse. But I don't want that for you. I don't want that at all. Turn your life toward Jesus. Pray with me right now."

"I have been prayin'—back there—while you preached. I can't do this anymore. I think it's time to go home to . . ." Her voice trailed off as she got up and disappeared behind the stage.

I stayed there for another fifteen minutes, but no one else came up to speak with me. So I went home and crawled into bed with Jean.

"How'd it go?" she asked through a sleepy haze.

"Okay," I said. "I guess."

I had gone there so excited. And yet the results were so minimal. No one was saved. I didn't pray with anyone. I never saw the young lady again. But perhaps seeds were planted. Perhaps someone's eyes were turned toward Christ and that person would be helped to salvation by someone else. I wasn't let down when I left, but I wasn't elated either. It had to be a matter of expectations, and mine were obviously too high. And yet, when you're dealing with what God can do, how can expectations ever be too high? Was the Lord really teaching me that I must expect less from him?

I doubt it. His Word says that he can do "exceedingly abundantly above all that we ask or think" (Eph. 3:20). That verse implies that we ought to have high expectations. So perhaps the lesson is not about our expectations, but about trusting the results to God.

Whether I got the lesson right or not, that certainly became a Christmas I never forgot.

REVISITING CALLI

Earlier I told you about Calli. She's the one who wanted to open her home to ladies dealing with unexpected and unwanted pregnancies, but no one came to take her up on her offer. There are a couple of other things I'd like us to consider about that situation. We originally looked at this unselfish woman in the context of prayers that seemed to be going unanswered. Here, let's consider her efforts in terms of what the Lord might be doing when he appears to be doing nothing at all.

When these things happen—when you work so hard for little or no result—it may be that the Lord is simply working on you. We often think that ministry happens as we help others; we minister to them. But often, and I say this from experience, *we* are the ones being ministered to—the ones being strengthened, or brought closer to our Savior, or having sins dealt with. Just as God's Word never returns void, so it is true with the experiences of our lives; they, too, are never useless. So, for Calli, it could very well be the Lord was working only on her and her husband and no one else.

But there's another thought. God also judges our motives. If we give to the church out of a desire to further the church's ministry, that's good in God's sight. If we give to get our name on a plaque or a building, that's sin in God's sight (although I don't want to discourage anything here). Since that's true, perhaps there are times when the motive to minister is what God is looking for; perhaps the motive and the preparations are all he wants for us at that time.

Perhaps the disappointment Calli and her husband experienced should not be seen as disappointment at all, but rather as the Lord taking us only so far and then giving us credit for being willing to go a bit farther. Calli and her husband had a sincere desire to minister to hurting women; God simply didn't open the door. They had to leave the results—or the apparent lack of results—in his hands.

But trusting God with the results of our efforts in ministry can be painfully difficult, especially when what seems to be a great success collapses into failure before your eyes. That's what happened with Camden.

CAMDEN

Camden was in his junior year of high school and sold drugs on the streets. By all measures, his life was careening downhill pretty fast. Although he wasn't thinking in these terms, his future held little more than fear, guilt, prison, and probably being murdered at an early age. But one day God seemed to reach down and pluck him out of the mire. Living with an uncle, Camden usually crawled out of bed long after the uncle was off to work. That morning, however, he was up early. Feeling restless, he dressed quickly and decided to go to a local coffee shop for breakfast. While waiting for a warmed Danish, he idly grabbed a piece of paper that had been left on the seat. It was a well-worn tract with our church's address on it.

After spending at least an hour reading and rereading that tract, Camden came to the church. The seed had definitely been planted in fertile ground. Within a few days he had taken Jesus Christ as his personal Lord and Savior and was beginning to repair the road ahead of him.

Of course, he stopped selling drugs. But he also became a dedicated student, going to classes as he was supposed to, doing his homework, being cooperative with his teachers. His uncle, a little confused by it all, observed that Camden was truly a changed young man.

I wasn't all that surprised when Camden began talking to me about a future in the ministry. He spent hours asking me and other members of our staff questions. He wondered what it would be like to pastor a church, what education he would need, what it was like to preach in front of hundreds of people, what it felt like to help change lives. He attended every Bible study he could, soaking up Scripture like a divinely inspired sponge. When he graduated from high school, he went to work for the church, trying to earn money to go to Bible college. He did any job we gave him and he did it diligently, sometimes working late into the night.

He became something of an answer man, particularly to the children. Being nearer their age, his answers seemed to mean more. And they were usually correct. He had obviously listened well.

Camden worked at the church for nearly two years, saving his money faithfully. Then one afternoon he came to me and said, "I'm quitting. Going to earn some money on the streets again. It'll be funny money, that's why I have to leave."

"Funny money" meant drug money.

I had never been so shocked. I am not usually at a loss for words. Often I think the Lord has filled me up with words, all of them eager for freedom; but at that moment my reservoir of words was totally empty. I stammered for a second as if to scrape a few from the reservoir walls. "How can you do this? You're a child of God. How can you walk away from him and reenter that kind of life again?"

He was surprisingly calm and unashamed. I know if I had professed Christ with all my heart for as long as he had and then decided to do something like this, I would have been ashamed. Camden wasn't. His demeanor was as calm as if he were telling me he wanted to take the afternoon off to go see a new Stallone movie.

Still desperately searching for the right combination of words to stave off this terrible plan of his, I told him that God would not be mocked in this way. If he truly was one of God's children, God would not allow him to profit from such a plan; whatever money he did make would be used against him somehow. I told him about people in Scripture having their heads cut off with their own swords. I was trying to be as graphic as I could. But I could tell from his face that nothing I said got through to him.

"No good will come of what you plan to do today," I finally reiterated, wishing I could somehow tie him up and stash him in the basement until this terrible moment passed for him. As he left the church, I prayed that the Lord would show him mercy.

Camden dropped out of sight for a week or so, then we saw him back on the street selling drugs. Less than four months later, he lay dead in the park, the victim of a drug deal gone wrong.

I often think about Camden. I wonder if he was saved—if, when he fell away so dramatically, the Lord ended his life to prevent his negative witness or to show him mercy, considering the path he was traveling. Of course, he may not have been saved at all. Perhaps the gospel seed had fallen on the thin soil where the love of money and the cares of this world burn the roots and kill the plant.

I hope I see Camden again one day, as I leave this world to be ushered into the presence of the King.

WHY ALL THE MYSTERY?

Why does all this ambiguity exist? Why are the signposts along our Christian journey visible only in dim light or the words seem to have several possible meanings? If God wants to speak to us, why doesn't he speak clearly?

I don't know. It would be the height of arrogance for me to try to explain God. He can explain himself if he wants us to know more than we do.

But there's one thing I do know: we see only a very small part of the puzzle God is putting together every day.

Have you ever seen an orchestral score? Each musical instrument has a different responsibility. They play different notes at different times as they make up the chords and facilitate the flow of the melody, or the rhythm and the accents. Others are heavy on mood, producing darkness, or a lightness, or sweetness. Yet all come together to make a powerful, unique, and sustained sound.

God is a planning God, and he orchestrates every-thing in accordance with those plans. As you can imag-ine, his plans include the whole world and affect all the people in it. Paul tells us that all national leaders govern at God's pleasure and that he directs their hearts (see Rom. 13).

In a very real sense, God is directing the greatest orchestra of all, and we are playing a part. Sometimes we might have the sustained melody, sometimes just an accent; sometimes we're there to set the mood. It's no wonder it's hard for us to discern the melody when we only have a few notes to play. For not only does God's plan affect the present, but it is also building a foundation for the future. Allow me to give you a few examples.

When Jacob presented his son Joseph with the coat of many colors, he was setting events in motion that saw national Israel grow from twelve brothers to about half a million people in the relative safety of Egypt's interior.

When Moses' mother put him in that reed basket as a baby, she was putting events in motion that would see the liberation of Israel from powerful Egypt, some four hundred years after Joseph.

An Indian brave named Squanto was taken as a slave from what would one day be called Massachusetts. When he was set free and eventually returned, now able to speak English, he helped the Pilgrims through that first winter. It was part of God's unfolding plan to establish America as a Christian nation.

When we see things occur in a vague sort of way, we must remember that we cannot see the complete musical score; we may have no idea what part we are playing in God's plan. When I preached at the Funky Ghetto, I had no way of knowing the actual effect I might have that night—or on whom. In fact, there are times I daydream about that event. It gives me encouragement about the rightness of that night, as if the excitement of the night's prelude was somehow justified by the result, instead of how anticlimactic the end of it seemed.

It could be that no one ever thought about the words of my sermon again, that the woman who said she was going to recommit herself to Jesus left the Funky Ghetto that night and never thought about Jesus again. But the Lord tells us that his word never returns void, that it accomplishes exactly what it sets out to do. God doesn't waste time, and he doesn't send his people out on senseless missions.

But I'll probably never know.

The point is I don't have to know. Unless I come across those people again, I'll never be part of their lives. I have to trust the results to God. My sights should be and are turned on people and events over which I have some influence, those things the Lord brings me in contact with on a daily basis.

LUMPS OF CLAY

There's another reason things sometimes proceed along in a vague sort of way. Have you ever watched a potter work with clay? In the beginning, she'll tear great chunks of clay away, slam what remains on the table, and knead it in an effort to begin the shaping process. Then she'll wet it, to make it more pliable, more easily molded and shaped as she gouges at it, tearing more away, smoothing a spot here, and slamming on additional clay there.

Sometimes the potter will turn it on a wheel, her hands squeezing and shaping, sometimes digging into it to make a radical change. She also uses tools for shaping, cutting, and edging. Then the clay object is fired for rigidity and strength. And when the potter is done, the completed work looks far different from the original lump of clay.

God calls himself the potter and us the clay. Every hunk of clay is a little different, just as we are different from our brothers and sisters. Even if we are fashioned for a similar use, the shaping process may be radically different.

So we see our lives as clay being shaped by a master craftsman. Sometimes the work is delicate: the introduction of an idea, a gentle realization. Other times it's more pronounced: the confrontation of a sin, the accusations of a loved one. Sometimes it's radical: an arrest, a divorce, the failure of a ministry, or something even worse. The Master is working with us to shape us for his purpose.

And when the time comes to think back on your ministry in the inner city, you'll see his loving fingerprints all over you, and you'll know beyond any doubt that you were working there as much for your spiritual benefit as the inner city's.

It's like doing a job and being paid twice—once when you actually do the work, and again when you look back on it all and see the Lord at work in you.

Can't beat *that* with a stick!

CHAPTER 12

Love
Will Cross
THE LINE

Jonah obeyed the word of the LORD and went to Nineveh.
Jonah 3:3 NIV

Jonah finally relented and obeyed the Lord. I look out upon Christendom and I see people far more willing than Jonah, far more eager to make a difference for their Lord. Currently they are making that difference in their homes, on their jobs, in their churches. Some are making more of a difference than others, but everyone who loves the Lord is at work in his kingdom to some degree.

My only request—and I believe this is God's call—is that you spend some of that time in ministry where it is needed beyond anything you could possibly imagine: the inner city.

In these pages we have met some of the inhabitants of the inner city. In a small way we have experienced moments in their lives, moments in their loves, and at times the fire of their rage. We've seen them as prisoners of their own fears, suspicions, and defeated spirits. Some of the fear, anger, and suspicion are justified—some of it not. Justified or not, it shouldn't be a reason to write them off.

After all, what were *we* like in *our* rebellion? Jesus met us where we were, and we must meet them where they are and bring them the good news of Jesus Christ.

And what good news that is—hopelessness to hopefulness, death to life, an existence of confused misery to one of divine purpose.

What is your ministry now? How are you using your gifts? I do not mean to belittle anything you are currently doing. If you're doing anything at all, you are on God's divine mission. But compare that to helping a little girl whose father has been murdered by gangs find the peace of Christ, or helping a young man replace drugs with Christ, or building a new classroom where women will learn the Christian way to take care of their children. The list of ministries needed in the inner city is endless, and they all end with taking people from the depths to the heights in Christ.

Oh, what a glorious mission!

And you can be a part of it. Start small—an hour a week, even less. But people's lives will be directly and eternally affected.

You've seen how the Lord has worked in our ministry over the last thirty-five years. Sometimes raising us up on a high pedestal so that his light might shine through us—once igniting the night sky so that his light might shine through us even more brightly later. Never once letting us down. Never once abandoning us. Never once allowing us to be overcome. Quite the contrary. I look back over those thirty-five years, and my eyes fill with tears at what the Lord has accomplished through his servants.

In thirty-five years what will you look back upon? Or even five years from now?

The U.S. Army calls you to "be all that you can be." Does God's army call us to be anything less?

You can put this book down in a few minutes and never think about it again. You're busy. Concerned people, busy people—people who would read this book in the first place are probably busy people. They are busy with their families, their churches, their lives, their ministries. Busy growing in the Lord, busy helping others grow. But are you *too* busy? If you are, if you're neglecting your family, your church, or your own spiritual growth in favor of a ministry, then it's actually time to ease off. But if you can find only an hour a week, even a few hours a month, you can accomplish miracles.

There's a saying, "If you want something done, give it to a busy person." Busy people know how to get things done. They know how to manage their time and fill the hours with "sixty minutes' worth of distance run," as Rudyard Kipling put it.

So, I'm appealing to you, my dear brother or sister in the Lord, to add the inner city to your "to do" list, just as the good Samaritan added the battered traveler to his.

God is calling you, just as he called the Samaritan, and just as he called Jonah to Nineveh. Of course, you have a choice as to how you might answer that call, but make no mistake, the call is there.

You can answer as the good Samaritan answered. You can cross the line to the wounded brother in the inner city. You can kneel down and assess the wounds, stop the bleeding, clean the wounds, pray, and assist him to a place where further assistance is available.

Or you can reply as Jonah did, by turning your back and running away.

Which of the two felt better when the day was done? Which of the two would look back on how the Lord used him with a holy pride and sense of divine accomplishment?

Maybe you're thinking that you'd like to get involved. You know how to now—a simple call to your church or an established ministry and you can begin the process of involvement. Don't put it off. Let the love of Christ motivate you. Feel the love he wraps you in every morning, and the love that lulls you to sleep each night. The love that called you from darkness into the light. The love that guides your footsteps into all good things. The love that placed him on the cross and compels you to help others.

I, and all the others at work in this vineyard, ask you to focus that love toward the millions of lost and dying in the inner city. Pick up your cross and carry it to the wall. Cross the line in Jesus' name.

ABOUT THE AUTHOR

George D. McKinney Jr., Ph.D., is the bishop of the Southern California Second Ecclesiastical Jurisdiction of the Churches of God in Christ, the largest black Pentecostal denomination in the country. He presides over sixty churches. He is the pastor and founder of St. Stephen's Church of God in Christ in San Diego, California. He has been a featured speaker at Urbana Mission Conferences and Promise Keepers. His ministry includes conducting conferences on the "Recovery of Family Life" and "Urban Ministry." He was selected as Mr. San Diego, Man of the Year 1995–96.

He earned a B.A. in sociology from the University of Arkansas in Pine Bluff, an M.A. in systematic theology from the Oberlin College Graduate School of Theology, and a Ph.D. from the California Graduate School of Theology.

He has authored several books including *The Theology of Jehovah Witnesses* and *Christian Marriage: An Act of Faith and Commitment.*